TOMORROW COMES

A teenager goes to bed and dies unexpectedly and inexplicably in her sleep. Her mother sets aside her grief to write a young adult novel, imagining the adolescent's point of view as she discovers the afterlife. What she finds affirms the value of the human connections we make ... For the young adult audience, Mebane presents a great alternative to the scores of vampire novels in which no one ever dies.

—*The US Review of Books*

Move over Harry Potter! If you are a fan of YA serials like **Harry Potter**, the **Hunger Games** and **Sweet Valley High**, then you simply must meet Emma, the heroine of **Tomorrow Comes** ... The best part of this debut novel is Emma's voice: bubbly, funny, likable and infinitely relatable, Emma is destined to become one of your best literary girlfriends along with Hermione and Katniss ... Great read for the YA and adult reader alike. A must have for any middle school classroom library.

—**Erin Maloney**, *Chicago Educator*

This is a great read for people who have wanted to try Alice Sebold's **Lovely Bones** but have been hesitant because of the violent storyline involved. The books ... both trace a family's journey through the grief process ... But **Tomorrow Comes** ... has a personal touch that **Lovely Bones** lacks. Author Donna Mebane is Emma's real mom writing about the death of her daughter. It is a raw, moving, emotional reading experience.

—**Portland Book Review** *(Kathryn Franklin)*

Tomorrow Comes is the first book I've read in many years that gives me a new way to think about death. Is it possible that we can continue to grow and evolve even after death? Do we maintain the relationships we had on earth?

—**Maureen Chambers**, *Psychologist*

I rarely "feel" so much when I'm reading, but I laughed at the bacon line, I cried in the hospital, my heart tightened along with Ben's, I felt the sun shining in Amsterdam, blinked back tears at the arrival of Duck, felt relief at the appearance of Aunt Pat, and smiled at the row of Gucci shoes.

    —**Sonia Vora**, *Award-Winning Author*

In the weeks following her death, Emma must learn how to balance her "before" life with her afterlife and learn how to tell her family that she is indeed OK ... An emotional novel about grief and the enduring power of love after death.

    —**Kirkus**

The book is a remarkable mix of dichotomies that you don't expect to live together — humor and sadness, truth and fiction — and simple, accessible language that speaks profound truths. Donna has just the right tone, humor, humility, and arc to make **Tomorrow Comes** appealing to a very wide circle of people.

    —**David Hunt**, *Owner, Town House Books & Café*

The premise of the book is novel and brilliant ... and I am convinced that the work not only will move readers in general, but will likely help those who are dealing with the loss of loved ones.

    —**Al Cave**, *Attorney*

Emma – I just finished your book. Oh, how I so believe that everything in the book is the way things really are for you. It brings me so much comfort to think that — to know that you are happy, a little excited, breaking the rules (haha), making friends, and even still throwing parties (haha). That's the Emma I know. If you could, I would like a visit in my dream please?

    —**Teague Wassel**, *Younger Sister of Emma's Friend Paige*

TOMORROW COMES

DONNA MEBANE

Geneva, Illinois ★ StarshineGalaxy.com

Donna Mebane

TOMORROW COMES

Geneva, Illinois / Starshine Galaxy / Revised Edition / 2014
254 pp / ISBN13 - 978-0-9857608-2-3 / ISBN10 - 0985760826
Library of Congress Control Number: 2014917101

As a work of reality fiction, *Tomorrow Comes* is based on and inspired by the true-life Emma Mebane. Learn more about Emma and her earthly journey at starshinegalaxy.com.

18 17 16 15 14   7 6 5 4 3 2 1

This book is dedicated ...

*... to all who love Emma
and to all who were loved by her.*

*... to the essential truth of a family – it shapes
what we become, and it becomes the shape of us.*

*... to the journey of becoming ... and the hope
that there is no end.*

**But, most of all, this book is dedicated to
Emma Lee Mebane.**

May she shine on, in all of us.

Contents

Chapters

Emma

Chapter 1

Emma opened her eyes. She was surrounded by a blaze of color, and she was filled with an overwhelming sense of peace. The sun streaming through her window was unusually bright, and her room was bursting with sensation. The pictures of family and friends that crammed her walls were so vibrant that they seemed almost alive.

She felt ... well, she felt joy. It had been kind of a stressful summer, one in which she found herself uncharacteristically worried about grown-up things, like what she was going to do for the rest of her life.

She still worried about her major, for example. Just five months ago, she wanted to be a teacher. She adored children and loved the idea of helping them grow, but she found out that it took a 3.5 GPA to get into the School of Education. *That's not going to happen,* she reflected at the time and began to explore other options.

She was thrilled that she had recently been accepted by the School of Art but, as she edged ever closer to the start of her sophomore year, she became progressively less sure that she had what it takes to be an artist. They loved her portfolio – her "body of work" as they referred to it in the acceptance letter – but privately she wondered if she was really that good.

As the baby of the family, she always felt that she had a lot to live up to. For all of her 19 years, she felt a little

overshadowed in the Brains Department by her older
sister and brother – Sarah and Ben – and in the Bravery
Department by her really older brother, Jason, who set
out on his own right after high school, when she was just
a little girl.

But this morning? This morning, all her worries
seemed to have disappeared overnight, and her confidence was soaring. This morning, for some reason, she
felt there was no mountain she couldn't climb.

How sappy is that? she thought with a start, but found
that even the dorkiness of thinking like a character from
The Sound of Music didn't dampen her mood.

She checked her iPhone. It was blinking 4:04. *Hmmm.
Doesn't feel like 4:04.*

As she stretched and tried to determine whether she
needed to get up yet, vivid images of her happiest
memories started flashing through her thoughts, beginning with her trip to London from which she had returned just eight days ago. She had traveled with Sarah
to visit her mom, who had accepted an international
work assignment starting in May.

~

She cried when Mom told her she was leaving for
London for six months. She found it very unfair that this
would happen just as her freshman year was ending. She
was so looking forward to being home from her first year
of college, slipping into being taken care of, and having
the kind of family fun that a small part of her worried the
proverbial clock was ticking away.

There was so much she wanted to say to keep her mom at home – *But what about me? ... I need you ... I want to be a carefree kid again, if only for the summer ... I want to snuggle with you in the mornings, and hug you every night ... I want to have pedi's and mani's with you ... I want to have you touch my cheek and tell me that everything is going to be all right, that I can be anything I want to be ...*

All she'd actually been able to blurt out is, *But who will make me bacon?* Duh. No wonder Mom laughed and simply said, *It'll be great. You can visit me in London anytime you want, and we'll have such fun.*

And Emma did visit, and she ended up having the time of her life.

~

It was late June when she flew to London with Sarah, and she was there for the first 10 days of Sarah's three-week vacation.

While she was there, she felt so grown up, and everyone treated her, at 19, exactly the same as Sarah, who was 30! She (well, Mom) bought her first real designer dress, she added two purses to her not-at-all-secret obsession (over 20 and counting), she rode like a rich commuter in a water taxi, and she ate all kinds of exotic food.

Very best of all? She could drink legally! No sneaking Icehouse beer through the basement windows in London as she had to at home. *I'll have what she's having,* she'd said on the plane as she pointed to Sarah and, lo and behold, the flight attendant brought her red wine. It's not like she was a lush or anything, but the simple pleasure of a beer with her pizza, champagne on the beach, and a Cosmo before dinner? *Heaven on earth!*

She was giddy with happiness when she and Sarah went to a bar (no fake ID required) with some of Mom's work friends. After an hour of fun, shots, and gossip, the cutest guy she had ever seen walked through the door, came straight toward her, lifted her onto her feet, kissed both cheeks (sooooo European!), and said in his perfect British accent, *Are you Emma Mebane? The Emma Mebane?*

She handled it perfectly. With all eyes on her, she replied, *Why, yes. And you are ...?* and when he replied, *Dan Gallo,* she vaguely recalled that her Mom had regularly talked about her work friend Dan and how hot he was.

Honestly, it was like something straight out of *Gossip Girl.* After the kiss that she saw was causing heads to turn in her direction, he sat right down at their table and proceeded to spend the night playing back stories that he had heard about Emma and Sarah over the years.

She had always been so horrified about how much her mother talked about her at work. *Emma Stories,* she'd call them. But that night in London she felt like a rock star. There was something about hearing the stories from a gorgeous older Brit that made them seem way more exotic than when her mom told everyone willing to listen.

When she and Sarah eventually returned to the flat, they hopped into bed with Mom and declared a new-found respect for her ability to know hot when she saw it! They giggled like school girls for hours, only partially because Emma and Sarah were just a tad tipsy.

The high point of the trip, without a doubt, was their puddle jumper to Ireland. Nothing in all the world prepared her for its absolute perfection. She told Mom that seeing Ireland was on her bucket list, and Mom replied, *You're too young to have a bucket list.* But she bought tickets to Ireland anyway.

They stayed at a really posh hotel and had lunch at a real Irish pub where she raised her very first real Guinness (if you didn't count Irish car bombs on New Year's Eve ... and she didn't). Toasting your sister with a Guinness on the sidewalk of a real Irish pub in the heart of Dublin with your mom capturing the moment with her iPhone for future generations? *Seriously!*

The next day they took a bus tour past the sea and into the country and, after figuring out that a 10-hour bus tour didn't mean sitting on a bus for 10 straight hours, she relaxed and had a blast.

She wouldn't have said that she believed in God. It's not that she didn't. She just never thought about it too much. But standing on the edge of a hill rolling with the purple of heather and looking down on a glittering lake with the breeze in your hair and the sun on your back, it was impossible not to feel that it was all part of some much larger plan.

∼

There I go again, she groaned. *Rolling hills and glittering lakes? What's gotten into me?* But even as she tried to clear her head, more memories crowded in.

It was like a movie of her life. Images ran through her mind like a slow train on the tracks by her house. She remembered family vacations – summers in the Outer Banks, the annual "theme" dinners at Grandma and Grandpa Mebane's, Cubs spring training in Arizona, and uncountable visits to Ocean City, New Jersey, which was close to where her mom had grown up and where her mom's parents and siblings all still lived.

She remembered "mini-vacations" like day trips to the shore, even in winter, to play miniature golf and get a slice of the best pizza on the planet at Mack and Manco's. And how many times did they have sleepovers in a resort not 10 minutes from home in Illinois just so that they could swim in the pool during the winter?

Even more vivid than the vacations were the memories of the in-between times – the every-day days. She remembered the way her dad would wake her up every morning until middle school singing, *Good morning, Emma! How are you today-ay?* She remembered the feeling of her foot connecting perfectly with a soccer ball, her hands executing a perfect pass in basketball.

She remembered the sparkle of her ruby red slippers, which she would wear day in and day out (frequent touchups with glue and glitter) from the time she was two until the time she was a "grown-up" kindergartner.

She remembered snuggling in the Mommy-Emma chair to watch movies by the fire. She could see each of her first days of school immortalized in the pictures taken with Ben until he went off to college, and then it was just her. Birthday parties and bedtime stories, breakfasts in bed, Daddy & Me dances, backyard bonfires and sleepovers on the trampoline ... each memory was crystal clear, and she could almost see every one of them all at once.

And she remembered Christmases.

Her family was gaga over Christmas. Everyone said that, but it really was ridiculous in her family. Opening presents was an all day ritual with only occasional breaks to munch on some of the "filler" presents (chocolate-covered pretzels, Bugle chips, and her personal favorite – *Starbursts)* that her mom insisted on getting to make everyone's number of presents come out even.

Every person had a particular place in the living room. Ben was always on trash detail, and Dad was always Santa. The present opening took forever – okay, partly because there were so many, but partly because her mom wrote little clues on all of them, and the family regularly collapsed with laughter trying to figure them out.

This was because: a) Mom never got around to wrapping until Christmas Eve and, as the night wore on and she got more tired, the notes made less and less sense, b) no one could really read her handwriting to begin with, and c) she made up who they came from. So, for example, one might say, *To my baby sister from her hunky bro. These are made for you-know-what'ing all over you.*

The clue sometimes made some kind of crazy sense after you saw the present (the aforementioned turned out to be boots, for example, which Ben had never even seen, let alone bought ... and *hunky?)* but more often than not, what barely made sense at 2:00 a.m. after one too many eggnogs was completely meaningless by morning. Even so, she still had some of the very "best" of the worst of them tucked away in her box of things most precious to her.

She wouldn't have changed one minute of any of her 19 Christmases. Although she always acted embarrassed, she was secretly kind of proud when friends would call at different points throughout the morning to ask what she got for Christmas and they hadn't really made a dent in their piles of presents yet. Even into the night, when her friends called to ask her to go out, she'd make up some excuse so she could stay home and squeeze every minute of fun out of this most wonderful of days.

There were the years they'd fought to be the one to wake up with the Santa pillow (which, because it was left at the foot of your bed on Christmas morning, guaranteed an extra present) or to be the one to get the "Big Stocking." There were the years that Sarah's tradition was to give her a beautiful dress, which she immediately put on and wore all day and even to bed on Christmas night.

She could see every ornament Grandma had made and every tree Dad had chopped down. Each year Mom said it was probably the biggest and best one ever, and only once had Dad poked a hole in the ceiling with a tree that *really was* the tallest one ever.

Last year, she and Sarah started a new tradition that (hopefully) Dad would keep funding (since it was "tradition," after all). She flew to Washington, D.C., as soon as Christmas break started so that she and Sarah could do some gift shopping and then together drive the 12 hours back home to Geneva.

Sarah had moved to D.C. three years ago and, though they talked and texted several times a day, she missed her terribly. Sarah had to drive all the way to Geneva every time she came home because usually she needed to bring those "little boys" – two "designer" dogs that had been pretty badly designed (and, truth be known, turned out to be not all that little either). She and Sarah listened to the new *Glee* Christmas CD the entire way home and laughed about nothing at all until their sides hurt.

~

As Emma's memories went clicking by, it occurred to her, not for the first time, what a charmed life she lived. She was loved, of that there was absolutely no doubt. And while she adored her friends and was told that she was someone who never met a stranger, she still had the best times and the most laughs with her family. She didn't often say that out loud because she was not some kind of geek who stayed in on Saturday nights. But she definitely lucked out when God gave out families.

Wait ... God again? She took a moment to try to pull all of this together but, now that the "movie" stopped, she was distracted from her thoughts by how intensely comfortable her bed felt.

True, she loved her bed more than any single place on earth. It was piled high with not one but three feather mattresses. She had at least a half-dozen feather pillows all around her, and the silky sheets and soft blankets were all selected for maximum comfort.

But this morning, she felt enveloped by a feeling of luxury she had never experienced. She recently (and quite cleverly, she felt) coined the phrase *Emm-azing* and this was definitely that. She felt like she might never be able to get out of bed again. The only thing missing was her ever present purring machine – her 15-year-old cat, Juice. Maybe she should just stay in bed a minute more until he came back from wherever he was uncharacteristically exploring.

Ah, but work (and Ben) awaited. Ben, who was not a risk taker, had definitely taken a risk three years ago when he recommended her for a job where he worked – a yummy and always busy bookstore and café – called (appropriately) *Town House Books and Café.*

At 16, she was the youngest person they ever considered, but it was also fair to say that she had not really established herself as particularly responsible. Nevertheless, Doug, the owner and manager, hired her, and she hadn't let him or Ben down. There were days, mind you, when she was pretty tired, having come home from some hearty partying, with barely enough time to brush her teeth and change her clothes before going off to work. But she always made it, and she wasn't about to risk being late just because her bed was unbelievable or her cat missed his morning snuggle for the first time ever.

~

When she stepped into the shower, she knew she made a wise choice to leave bed. The water felt like dew drops caressing her skin and, if she didn't know better, she might have thought she was in some kind of mystical rain forest with a steaming waterfall awakening her every pore. Once again, she had to force herself to end this part of what had, until today, been a pretty uneventful morning routine.

As she wiped away the steam in the mirror and took a hard look at herself, she was amazed at what she saw. Most people found her pretty and, the truth is, she mostly thought they were right. She did like the crystal blue of her eyes and the slight upturn of her nose. She thought her mouth was a little too small, but if she parted her lips just so, she could achieve a certain poutiness that the boys seemed to like.

She was always working on losing 10 pounds – all, it seemed to her, in her thighs – but, in the plus column, she loved her boobs and had a nice flat stomach. On her best days, she felt she could hold her own with all but the most beautiful of her friends and, though she never had a real boyfriend, she always had her fair share of dates.

Her one recent challenge was that just before she went to Europe, she dyed her hair a reddish brown in the hopes of looking more Irish. BIG mistake. She hated it, but her hairdresser said it would be too hard on her hair to try to dye it back to her natural blonde.

Incredibly, as she looked at herself now, she realized that her hair was as beautifully blonde as it had ever been and, when she smiled back at the image in the mirror, she positively glowed. While they were in London, Sarah gave her what was left of some new kind of shampoo that was supposed to bring out natural highlights. *Note to self: Buy more! Immediately.*

Her sense of peace and immeasurably deep satisfaction stayed with her as she sorted through her new London outfits to find one befitting her hair. Her one slight annoyance was that all the clocks in her room still said 4:04.

Dad? she yelled, *What time is it?*

No answer. She vaguely recalled that he said something about going into work for a meeting this morning. Speaking of charmed and while she was feeling so mellow, she took a moment to reflect on her dad.

She loved her dad in a way that she knew was special. He was quirky, yes. But he let her be who she was. More than that, he was on her team, front and center, and he actively helped her become who she wanted to be. One time, he quit what she assumed was a great job so he could work at home to be with her, which made her life immensely better. After experimenting with getting her to after-school activities via a horrifyingly embarrassing kid taxi service – *Wheels R Us* – suddenly her dad was there to chauffeur her, and there he had stayed. Her house became the place to be after school, and over the years her friends came to love "Rodney" almost as much as she did.

As she finished dressing and came downstairs, she saw that, as usual, Dad left out half a grapefruit and a not-too-stale-to-eat-but-too-stale-to-sell-to-customers scone from Town House. *Man, I am so happy.*

As she ate her grapefruit (and, yes, broken record – it was scrumptious), she sang a line from *Wicked*, her favorite musical. *I simply couldn't be happier,* she belted, and she danced around the kitchen.

Wicked was a favorite family musical and also a favorite family joke because Emma had insisted, on the way to seeing it the first of four times, that the title of the musical was pronounced *Wickt* (one syllable, like the past tense of a candle wick). Then, she compounded that little snafu by insisting (fabricating!) that her teacher told her that this was the right way to say it.

As she got ready to leave for work, she left a note for her dad to check the clocks, grabbed her keys, and started toward the garage. Just as she was about to open the door, she heard a scratching at the sliding glass doors to the backyard behind her. *Surely Dad didn't leave Monty outside.* Monty had never been a dog who loved the outside and especially when it was hot. It had been swelteringly hot since the 1st of July and today, the 8th, it was supposed to break 100. *Yuk.*

She started toward the back door and froze. There, scratching to get in, was not the smelly, farty, wheezy old Monty that she expected. There, scratching to get in was Monty's brother, Duck, everyone's favorite – the beloved, snuggable, loving and lovable, and now-nearly-three-years-dead best dog ever!

Sarah

Chapter 2

The trip started out with such promise. Although it had been raining, almost the second the plane touched down, the sun came out. It was as though Amsterdam had showered and then put on its best party dress just for them.

You're so lucky, the cabbie said, just as they pulled up to the Okura Hotel and right before he ripped them off by charging 15 Euro too much. *It's been raining for days.*

You're so lucky, the concierge said, as he opened the door to the most magnificent hotel either of them had ever seen. *Beautiful weather.*

We are so lucky, Sarah and Mom thought, as they opened the door to a huge room with a panoramic view of the gorgeous city. *We couldn't be happier*, Sarah sang, as she danced around the room singing out a song from her favorite musical.

Sarah and her mom were living the life. Unlike Emma, who had to be convinced, Sarah was instantly excited about her mom's assignment to London. Never one to walk away from opportunity, Sarah had been thinking she'd like to travel more, and there was no time like the present to start!

She and Emma experienced London and Ireland in a way that made her thirst for more, and the Amsterdam/ Bruges leg was by far the most exotic they had planned for her three-week vacation.

Her only regret was that Emma would not be a part of it. She and Mom pleaded with her to stay – the party was always better with Emma. She laughed to herself as she thought about her up-until-now best vacation ever.

~

Last year, Mom took them on an all-girls week to Cape Cod to celebrate her 30th birthday. The house they rented was magnificent (you gotta love a house that has a name – *Sandy Toes!*). It was several stories high and sat on a cliff overlooking the ocean. Sarah, her mom, her mom's sisters – Carol and Susan – and her cousin Katy arrived on a Tuesday, and Emma was scheduled to fly in on Friday so she wouldn't miss any classes. Amazingly(!?), Emma's Thursday classes were cancelled, and Emma called and begged Mom to change her ticket to Thursday. Mom pretended to protest for a bit (*honestly, Emma, 200 bucks so you can be here, what, 10 minutes earlier?*). But everyone knew she would give in.

Yep, the party didn't really get started until Emma arrived. And, sure enough, she burst in like a one-man band, bringing nonstop laughter and shimmering sunlight (literally – it had been cloudy and Octobery the day before).

There were probably not two sisters on earth who were seemingly more different than Sarah and Emma. Though both had blonde hair and blue eyes, Emma's only-thought-by-her-to-be-extra 10 pounds was more like mostly-tucked-away-but-still-there 30 pounds on Sarah. Where Emma had always been glittery with sparkly dresses, designer sunglasses, and whatever jewelry was the current fashion statement, Sarah preferred a "professional" look even before she became a professional.

While Emma could pull together a party spontaneously in under five minutes and, within ten, the music was blaring so loud you couldn't hear yourself shout, Sarah liked to plan little get-togethers during which there was much friendly discussion about world events or the latest Oprah book. Equal amounts of laughter and camaraderie, but decidedly different kinds of fun.

Emma saw school primarily as a venue, albeit a little restrictive, for being with her friends. (She once, when Dad asked which was her favorite class, considered for several minutes before responding that it had to be biology. Pleased, Dad asked why. *Because,* gushed Emma, *it has Kevin and Paige and Doni and Mel and Taylor AND Zack.*)

Sarah saw school primarily as a wonderful world of learning. She earned her Ph.D. in psychology in record time and was seriously sad because she couldn't legitimately think of a reason to stay in school longer.

No one would mistake Emma for a genius, but Sarah really was one. She was almost a child prodigy in math and after a rigorous testing and interview process (and much to the surprise and dismay of her mom who wasn't prepared to part with her), she was accepted at age 13 to IMSA – the Illinois Math and Science Academy – a prestigious, residential high school.

One of the stories the family loved to tell was about the time Emma was eight, when she and Mom ran into one of Ben's grammar school teachers. Ben, no slouch himself academically, was then in middle school and the teacher asked if he was still getting straight A's. *Oh, yes,* answered Mom, *he's doing very well.*

Didn't his sister go to IMSA? asked the teacher, and Mom confirmed that she had. Emma, always just a little uncomfortable in the presence of teachers, but sensing a compliment, brightened up, kind of puffed out her chest a bit and chimed in, *I did???*

Oh, Emma! (Wrong sister.)

On the other hand, over the years, Emma developed her own Ph.D. in social skills. She hadn't started out popular as a kid, and it had never been her goal to become so. That said, though Emma always had friends, she definitely moved up the food chain over the years and, by high school, she was a part of the crowd envied by all.

The truly wonderful thing about Emma, though, was that she really didn't seem to notice. She still hung out with friends she made throughout the years and had special times with them all.

She had a knack for putting people at ease and, though she lived her fair share of drama, she was rarely the cause of it. If asked to pick one word to describe Emma, most people would say that she was quite simply, *FUN.*

She rarely questioned others, and what her parents often feared was naiveté, her friends believed to be a pure and honest sincerity. Emma believed what people told her because they told her it was so. She got no pleasure out of questioning motives and usually lost at mind games.

Despite their differences – or perhaps because of them – Emma and Sarah thoroughly enjoyed each other and, given a choice of anyone else to hang with, they would almost always pick each other.

Their bond started as a fascination with each other from nearly the day Emma was born. There were nearly 12 years between them, and Sarah was overjoyed to have a little sister. She took every chance she could to remind everyone that she was prime babysitting age. She would beg to hold Emma and feed her and take her for long walks. It wasn't long before Emma's face would light up as soon as Sarah walked in the room. *Rah* was Emma's first word.

No wonder that these days Sarah's friends called her the baby whisperer – the one who could calm any child and in whose arms any baby in the room eventually ended up. Time spent with Emma taught her how to love a child and developed in her a gentle patience that even the crankiest babies could sense.

Emma had only been two when Sarah moved away to live the school year at IMSA. Sarah worked hard to stay connected. She went home to visit "the kids" (the way she affectionately referred to her much younger siblings) every chance she got – almost every weekend and, once she could drive, often a couple of times during the week as well.

Sarah would often hatch crazy, complicated plans so that she wouldn't have to miss the milestones of Emma's childhood. *Okay, so if I slip out of my last morning class a little early and, if I catch all green lights, I can be home just in time to watch Emma's part of the kindergarten circus play.*

Then, I'll have time to hug her and congratulate her before I speed back for my calculus study group.

Throughout those early years, a trip to see Sarah was the high point of Emma's social life. Emma never missed a sibling weekend at IMSA and, because Emma was one of the youngest siblings, she was an instant favorite with everyone. Who could resist that dimpled smile, those chubby cheeks, and her even-as-a-toddler unique fashion sense?

It seemed that, from birth, Emma could charm anyone she met, and Sarah, just like her mom, would proudly tell Emma stories to anyone who would listen. They flipped roles when Emma was in middle school and it was family day – the day when each middle-schooler was allowed to invite an adult to shadow them at school for the day. When most of the other kids had parents, aunts and uncles, or grandparents, Emma seemed to be one of the few with a cool grown-up sister!

Over time, Emma's visits to Sarah's high school became visits to college and then visits to grad school, and Sarah's trips home for kindergarten events and elementary school solos became cheering at soccer games, taking pictures before dances and at graduations and, finally, last year, visits to Emma's college.

For most of their lives, Sarah thought of herself as the teacher and Emma the student and, indeed, her relationship with Emma contributed significantly to her chosen career as a psychologist. Emma regularly sought her advice and, at an early age, Sarah realized that she gave pretty good counsel and did it in a way that stemmed from genuine caring. And so she went on to develop her big sister instincts through formal education.

In recent years, their relationship shifted and, as Emma became more confident and sure of herself, she would often give advice that helped Sarah grow in the areas of Emma's expertise – in fashion and fun and bouncing back from setbacks.

Sarah could vividly recall an incident where she marveled at Emma's reaction. One of Emma's very best friends, Cayla, was having a tough time with money. As her 16th birthday approached, it didn't look like it was going to be a great one. Emma decided that she would do something very, very special for her, and she searched the internet to find a time when Cayla's favorite group, *30 Seconds to Mars*, might be playing in Chicago.

As luck would have it, they were coming to town in two months and, despite the fact that the StubHub ticket prices were outrageous, Emma dug into her savings without hesitation and purchased two tickets. After much begging and promising to be careful, Emma and Cayla got permission to take the train to Chicago and, as the big day approached, they were beyond excited.

They planned and re-planned the day and when it finally came, they took hours together trying on clothes, picking out jewelry, and getting their hair and makeup just right. As they came downstairs to say goodbye to Mom and Dad, Emma picked up the tickets and suddenly stilled.

Wait, she said. *What's today's date?*

The 19th, Dad promptly answered.

Aw shit, Emma sighed, momentarily forgetting that swearing was not something she did in front of her parents. *These are for last night.*

Everyone stopped in their tracks with looks of sheer horror until suddenly Emma started to giggle. *Oh, well,* she said, hugging Cayla. *We look totally hot, and we'll take our iPods and listen to the band all night and we'll have a blast.* And darned if Cayla didn't start laughing, too, and they left holding hands looking for all the world on the cusp of having the best time ever.

And that was Emma being Emma. She was like the little toy that hit the wall and backed up and turned and went into a different direction. Yes, there was much to be learned about life and love and joy from her baby sister and, over time, Sarah became as much a student as she was a teacher.

Both were devastated when Sarah had to move to Washington, D.C., to take her first real job. They talked or texted several times a day. They were each the first the other would call if something good or bad happened. Sarah continued to plan her precious vacation time around Emma, and Emma would always stay home at least one weekend night if Sarah was in town.

Now that Emma was becoming an adult, Sarah was overjoyed that they could share their deepest thoughts, fears, and dreams. In a weird kind of way, they were two parts that together made a fabulous whole. The Mebane sisters.

~

And now here Sarah was in Amsterdam without Emma. It just didn't feel right somehow. Still, they agreed to facetime the second Emma got home from work that night, and Sarah promised to take tons of pictures. Speaking of taking pictures, time was wasting as they only had three short days to explore.

Let's go, Sarah called to Mom, who was still discovering freebies in the outrageously huge bathroom.

As Sarah and Mom walked out the door, they were welcomed by a blaze of color and an invigorating sense of adventure. They wanted to see and do everything. *Which way?* Mom asked and, as they tried to pick a lane from the indecipherable map, they realized that it really didn't matter because any way would lead to something they had never experienced.

They giggled at the signs they couldn't pronounce and marveled at how little they recognized in the store fronts. Though they were starved, they couldn't read the menus in the windows of restaurants, so they followed their noses right into a total dive of a place with ripped vinyl stools and a line out the door.

Genuine meat, might have been what the father at the counter said and, when they'd agreed vigorously that it was what they wanted, he shook his head *No* just as vigorously, tore a few hunks off something on a spit, proudly rolled them up in something pita-like *(Genuine Greek,* maybe?), and handed it to them with great flourish. Whatever it was, it was the most delicious thing they'd ever tasted, and they moaned with pleasure after each bite.

Do you think we could get more? Mom asked, but Sarah held firm. They had dinner reservations that evening at a TripAdvisor-inspired "best bet," and there were still French fries to find somewhere. (Everyone said that the fries in Amsterdam were second only to those in Bruges and, both being fry connoisseurs, they were inspired to find out!). *We'll come back tomorrow,* Sarah promised and, after hugs all around, they left the hole-in-the-wall with promises, likely not understood, to return.

As they wandered down the cobblestone streets in Amsterdam, they quickly (after being nearly flattened twice) found the walkers sidewalk (versus the bikers sidewalk). And, after sharing a plate of what they agreed had to be second-to-none fries, they turned a corner and there, sprawling ahead of them, was a street market with blocks and blocks of gaily decorated stalls, crowds of what appeared to be genuine Amsterdamians, booths of wooden shoes, and tulips and cheeses and chocolates, and smells that, despite being sprinkled with an occasional whiff of pot, made their mouths water all over again.

I am the kid in the proverbial candy shop, Sarah sighed, and she and Mom filled their bags with exotic fruits, cheesy (but colorful!) gifts, and fresh tulips (when in Rome!). They went into a "coffee" shop just so they could say they could have bought hashish if they wanted to and practically cried with the sheer joy at the random turns that brought them to this place.

They expressed their utter contentment, often in words, but also in the smiles permanently placed on their faces. *I am so happy,* Sarah said, and her words were almost profound in their simplicity. *I feel such joy. I don't ever want this feeling to end.*

Sadly, they didn't get even half way when they realized they'd have to cut this part of their adventure short. Sarah arranged to join a bike tour (her current favorite way to learn about a new city), and they had to separate. Hard to believe it was still morning. They already crammed so much into their first few hours and were filled to the brim with the lovely possibilities the next few days held.

As they said goodbye and made arrangements to meet back at the room, somewhere a clock was striking 11:00 a.m. They hugged. As they stood on the street with the hustle and bustle of another world all around them, they were overflowing with gratitude (to a higher power? to Mom's company?) that they were together in this truly heavenly place. They both felt like they wanted to freeze this moment for all time, that somehow they would never again be as happy as they were right then.

Don't go, Mom said suddenly. *Stay with me.*

Sarah glanced at her watch. 11:04, it read. The happiness she felt just seconds before fled, and she suddenly felt cold and almost afraid.

I will if you want me to, she replied.

Sarah felt instinctively that if they parted, something would be lost forever, something that they would never be able to regain. She thought fleetingly and inexplicably of Emma, half a world away and still safely asleep in her bed.

As she watched, her mom shook her head a little, and the moment passed. *No, you go on. It'll be fun, and I'll see you soon. Maybe you can make us some dinner money,* she smiled, *in the red light district.*

You're sure? Sarah asked, uncertain.

Of course, Mom replied. *Plus, I have some work to do.* She gave Sarah's hand a little squeeze, turned, and walked away.

Emma

Chapter 3

Emma was not the kind of girl to question something that made her happy. Still, she was torn between rushing to receive what she knew would be the best dog kisses ever and pausing to try to sort things out.

Maybe it isn't really Duck, she considered, but even through the glass doors she could hear the happy half hums, half squeals that were pure Duck talk.

OK then, maybe he didn't really die, she speculated.

~

After piling into the car to bury Duck in the dog park where he spent his best non-loving-with-his-people time, they all gathered under a secluded shade tree to say their tearful goodbyes. She vividly remembered Dad's speech (partly because it was so beautiful, and partly because she kind of "borrowed" sections of it later for a paper of her own about sadness and death).

Dad talked about the hundreds of hours he had spent in the park with Duck and how Duck traveled every square inch checking for exotic smells, small critters, and new places to lift his leg. Dad talked about the anxiety he always felt, worrying that, when he called out to Duck that it was time to go home, Duck wouldn't come back.

He started to tear up when he talked about imagining the worst and wondering what he would do if there ever came a day when Duck didn't return. They all started to cry when Dad said he always got to thank God because Duck always did manage to find his way back. Until he didn't ...

Wonderful wiggly Duck had the biggest heart of any dog EVER. But way, way before his time, Duck's big heart stopped working right and, though he survived the operation, he was just too weak to bounce back ... to "come out of the woods" one more time and go home. And so they buried him there on a hill with a view of the river so that he could look out over his dominion and protect the place he loved so much.

~

They did bury him, didn't they? It was Duck under that rock high on that hill, wasn't it? For one terrifying instant, Emma thought that maybe she was about to have a *Pet Cemetery* moment and that the Duck who was now practically pleading with her to let him in would go all zombie on her and smell bad and try to bite her eyes out.

Admonishing herself to step back off the ledge (*this is real life, Emma*), she opened the door. Duck bounded in and practically knocked her over. It seemed he couldn't wag his tail or wiggle his body enough to show the kind of love he was wanting to show – love that would have built up inside him for the three long years he had been ... well ... away.

She fell back on the green couch (a source of great pride to all that they had a green leather couch in the kitchen of all places, and dogs and people alike were always jockeying for position on it). She definitely felt a bit dazed but, percolating under the confusion and managing to bubble to the top of her many feelings was the sheer pleasure she felt to see Duck again.

~

Duck was the dog version of the love of her life. They all met him when he was three days old, before he even opened his eyes. Ten Christmases ago, Dad gave Mom an IOU for a German shorthaired pointer puppy because they had so admired the four that his boss owned.

When the boss's dog had a litter, the whole family went over to see them. All nine of the puppies had clever names corresponding to their markings. Mom instantly was drawn to Diamond Back (who eventually became Monty) but, at some point, closed eyes and all, Duck (owing to a duck-shaped marking on his side) found his way to Ben, climbed up on to his lap and wiggled his way into Ben's heart.

Although the hallmark moment was briefly spoiled when Duck shat on Ben's pants, that day started a love affair that lasted until the day Duck ... went away. Ben loved Duck and Mom loved Ben so, being Mom, she decided they should buy both of them (same way Sarah got those two "little boys") and Dad, being Dad, agreed.

~

As Duck ran to his toy box, picked out an appropriate gift and raced through this house on a hunt for, she assumed, Ben, Emma thought about how the whole family mourned his loss for months.

What Emma missed most was the way Duck was always a part of whatever was going on. All of her family members were big snugglers, and Saturday mornings were the best. Ben had to work early most Saturdays and, when he got up, Duck would come bounding upstairs, leap on her mom and dad's bed and lay down as close as he could possibly get to "his people."

Then he dog-purred to let you know he was happy, and he'd nudge you with his paw until you couldn't help but love with him. The only way to stop scratching him was finally to get up and start your day. Otherwise he would continue with nonstop nudging and pleading and purring.

Duck was usually wherever the action was and, since most of the action was often with her, he'd be a near constant companion when he wasn't with "his boy." He jumped with her friends and her on the trampoline, boogied to *Dance, Dance Revolution,* and howled his accompaniment to party music.

Turns out Duck wasn't the best retriever in the world. She laughed out loud remembering the time the fridge broke and they had put all the frozen stuff in the back yard in the snow to keep it from spoiling. Mom forgot and let Monty and Duck out. She realized her misstep within minutes, but not before Monty had hunted down a $75 roast and was happily munching away on it.

Duck, on the other hand, knew it wasn't right to eat the spoils so, when he came in, he proudly deposited his find at their feet. Sadly, it was a bag of frozen corn, but they all praised him as though it was a pheasant or a quail or even a steak or frozen chicken.

～

Just then Duck returned looking slightly dejected because he hadn't found the rest of the family. Emma invited him up onto the couch and there they sat for several minutes, both of them feeling such peace that, for whatever the reason, they had found each other again. Emma *loved* (the Mebane term for scratching, petting, and snuggling with the dogs, as in, *I think Duck needs some "love"*) as hard as she could with him, and Duck loved back with every inch of his being. It was a magical few minutes and Emma wished that they could go on forever just like they were at that moment.

Eventually, Emma roused herself, stood up, and gave Duck a final kiss on the head. *I'm sorry, Ducky, but I have to go to work. I'll see Ben, though, and will he be glad to see you! You'll be here when I get back, right?* At the sound of his boy's name, Duck thumped his tail harder.

Would you like to hear his voice? Would you promise to stay here if Ben told you to? Emma asked.

She grabbed her phone and dialed Town House's number. She got a weird whining sound and hung up to redial. She got the same whining sound and, as she looked at her phone more closely to see what number she dialed, a voice came on saying, *Have you forgotten the rules? Please hang up and try music ...*

What in the world is going on today? she wondered. First the clock stopped, and now the damn phone wouldn't even make a call right.

She turned to Duck. *Stay,* she said. *I really, really mean it. Do NOT go away again, or I'll be really mad. Do you hear me?* Duck thumped his tail, which she took as a sign of agreement.

With one more quick pat on the head and scratch behind the ear, she started out to the garage, hoping nothing else weird would delay her from getting to work and telling Ben about the most amazing thing EVER.

Ben

Ben's anxiety was increasing. As he continued to set up for the lunch time rush, he glanced at his watch again. 10:40. Where was she? Customers were already lining up and, once they were officially open for lunch, the patio would fill up quickly. Emma knew that, and Friday was her only patio day this week. Patio days were "money" days. You were busy from the second you walked in until the kitchen blessedly closed at 4:00. But if you were patio on a good day, you could make 200 bucks, and today looked like it was going to be a very good day.

Though Ben tended to think of Emma as on the unreliable side, he had to admit she had never let him down at work. Many a time she came close, and many a time he had to bail her out of some situation or another just hours before they'd both have to get up. How many times had his phone rung at 2:00 or 3:00 in the morning? He longed to ignore it, at least once or twice, but he never did. *Are you awake?* she'd always ask. *I am now,* he'd always reply.

~

A few years ago, there was a terrible accident the next town over. Several teenagers, just 15 and 16, went to a party, got sloppy drunk and were chased out by the over-20's who were hosting the party. It was in the dead of winter and, feeling sorry for them stumbling down the road, one of the party goers stopped on her way home and offered them a ride. Soon after, they skidded into a tree, no one was wearing seat belts, and everyone in the car was seriously injured. Mothers and fathers everywhere were horrified.

Soon after this accident, Mom sat Emma down and had a long talk with her. *If you ever need a ride home and I mean EVER, no matter what time of the night, no matter where you are, you call home. We'll come and get you with absolutely no questions asked. I mean it!*

Emma was appropriately impressed and, though it didn't curtail her social life, from then on, she called home if anything got even a little out of control. Only problem was, she interpreted Mom's advice pretty liberally and always called Ben whenever she needed a ride. It seemed safer to call Ben than to face the wrath of Mom. Though she was pretty sure Mom would keep her word and not ask any questions, Mom had a way of letting you know she was unhappy without saying anything at all.

No, far better to tap into brotherly love and, anyhow, it was way more fun to cap off a night with friends in the company of Ben.

Although Ben always grumbled, the truth was he didn't mind all that much. Ben was kind of an introvert, and he definitely played by the rules. Emma was the dictionary definition of an extrovert and definitely didn't play by the rules, and so in a way he lived a little vicariously through her.

He had friends, for sure. In fact, he had lots of them. But he didn't drink and rarely partied. Mom liked to tell the *Tale of Two Siblings* by describing parent's weekend this year at ISU.

Ben stayed at home to mind the fort. Mom, Dad and Emma had a wonderful time going to dinner Friday night, tailgating before the big football game, and rooting the home team on to a rare victory before dinner Saturday night. The high point of the weekend (at least according to Dad) was to be a rousing concert of dueling pianos.

They all had such a good time together, but during dinner, Emma got increasingly fidgety. *Um, about the dueling pianos,* she said.

Won't it be awesome? asked Dad.

Well, sure, she said. *I mean I totally love you guys so, so much. And I love pianos. And I LOVE dueling. It's just that ...* She hesitated for dramatic effect. *It's just that there's a frat party tonight, and it's to benefit the arthritis foundation. And I really worry a lot about arthritis ...*

Again, she tailed off and tried to put on her best it's-so-not-about-the-beer face. Dad, who could rarely resist giving in to what Emma wanted and could never do so when she had that face on, laughed and said of course she should do what she could about arthritis, and they had kissed and hugged and promised to meet bright and early the next day for brunch.

In the meantime, Ben, who was 200 miles away in a huge house all to himself, asked if he could have a few friends over. His parents readily agreed to the request (one that Emma would never have been so forthcoming as to make nor, had she slipped up and made it, would ever have been granted). And Ben did not disappoint. When Mom called to check in, she could hear laughter in the background.

Sounds like you're having fun, she said and Ben replied that they were having a blast, but that he had to go because they were in the middle of a *Star Wars Monopoly* tournament.

So, here was Emma, 18 and in the very same town with her parents, somehow finding a way to ditch them to party with her friends (all in the name of arthritis, of course, so there's that), and there was Ben, over 21, miles away with the whole house to himself playing *Monopoly.* Go figure!

Unlike the instant love between Sarah and Emma, Ben and Emma's now unshakeable bond developed more slowly over the years. Ben was committed to doing things right and, as a child, Emma had a knack for doing everything wrong.

One of the family's most treasured items was one of their extremely rare video recordings. (Dad, for some reason understood only by him, preferred to take still pictures and "fill in the moments" instead of videotaping. Mom, being technically challenged in all things, had to defer to him.) The video was classic Ben and Emma.

Ben, nearly four, is busy with all things Ben, puttering around, putting things away, studiously building a tower out of blocks. Emma, 18 months, is amusing herself with a flower petal. Lying between them is a new gym mat that Ben had gotten for his gymnastics class at preschool. At one point, Mom's voice chimes in, asking Ben to show them what he'd learned. Ben runs over and executes two flawless somersaults. The family claps and cheers and

Ben, never, ever one to like center stage, pulls his shirt over his head and tells them to quit it.

Emma, who always does her best with an audience, senses an opportunity and toddles over to the mat. *Can you do one, Emmaline?* coos Mom. Emma grins, claps her chubby hands, and promptly flops down and scrunches her body around, turtle-like a few times. *Hurrah,* the family claps and cheers. Ben is astounded and more than a little annoyed. *That's not right,* he protests. *That is NOT a somersault.*

There is general hubbub for a few minutes, with Mom trying to soothe Ben and Emma continuing to flop around and then cheer for herself. Unable to restore order on camera, the video is turned off and, when it comes back on, the mat is gone, Emma has returned to her flower petal, and Ben is reading a book on Mom's lap. (No still picture could have filled in all those moments!)

Ben couldn't remember when his feeling of tolerance of Emma, because she was his little sister, turned to amused affection and finally crossed over to a deep and vital love. He suspected the seed had always been there, watered over time by an overwhelming sense that she needed him and the protection that only a big brother could provide.

It seemed the journey to love for Ben on Emma's part was much faster. The family was photo happy, and there were several early ones with Emma looking up at Ben adoringly. Long about fifth-grade (Ben) / second-grade (Emma), Ben started putting a protective arm around her in the first day of school pictures that Dad always insisted on. And for the last one they took together, as he was entering senior year and she her freshman year, it was clear from her idolizing gaze and his adoring look down at her that the journey for both was complete.

That was an interesting year. For the first time in several years, they both were in the same school and, over time, she became legitimate friends on her own with some of his friends. She was so pretty and vivacious – some said she shone like a star – that she drew people to her, but some of those people were users who wanted nothing more than the proverbial notch on their belt. Ben stepped in many times and warned away people who could have hurt her.

Over time, Emma came to trust Ben with her whole being and regularly sought his advice on everything from music to homework to friends. Her orbit was a bit dazzling for him, and he was more than a little proud of his special place in her life.

The strength of their relationship had caused him to go way, way out on a limb and suggest that Doug consider her for a position at Town House. After Ben's introduction, she got the job purely as a result of her personality and her eagerness alone, given that her previous work experience was one week at the local movie theater. And, truth be known, despite his protests of their extreme differences, the Town House family had a special fondness for Ben and an unspoken hope that she would be, at least in part, a female Ben.

Doug asked Ben to train Emma, and he did so with extreme trepidation. But she wanted to make them all proud and threw herself into work with every ounce of her considerable enthusiasm and charm. They were all amazed at how quickly she learned. She instantly endeared herself to the wait staff, the cooks were forever flirting with her, and even the "old biddiest" of the regulars quickly learned to look past the itty bitty diamond in her nose.

She quite simply brightened up the place and, over time, Ben came to appreciate that what she may have lacked in doing things right, she more than made up for by doing things with gusto. Even though his efficiency enabled him to still be the top earner, within a few months she regularly beat him in percentages (which despite his frequent explanations she could never quite calculate herself!).

They worked to stay connected when he moved to California for two years of college. They texted frequently and talked on the phone regularly. Because he could only now protect her with words, their talks became more open, and the topics of their conversation deepened. Ben discovered that what he and others mistook for a lack of depth was really just a unique way of seeing the world. Emma's glass was always half full, and she refused to accept or even see anything that might shake her fundamental belief that life was good.

Ben returned home, having run out of money the Christmas before Emma went away to ISU. Much to everyone's surprise, she had accumulated enough credit to graduate high school early. So, at about the same time, Town House became more than just a summer job to them, and they both threw themselves into work with passion and a new sense of commitment.

It seemed to him that Emma grew up over those months in front of his very eyes. Although she still liked to have a good time, more often than not this involved dinner with friends, an evening with family, or time spent with Hannah – the first Town House baby and a source of pure joy for Emma.

They had all driven her to college, and she had cried like a little girl when they left. In truth, Ben wasn't sure she'd make it and, though she got decent grades her freshman year, he still had his doubts. In the spring, Emma's innocent acceptance of the good intentions of others failed her, and she was date raped by someone she had called a friend.

The rape caused absolute havoc in the family, and they all kicked into high gear to help her through it. Mom immediately arranged for her to see a counselor, and both she and Sarah were helping her move from horror and helplessness to outrage and action. Dad and Ben wanted names, dates and serial numbers. Dad, in particular, was encouraging her to think about going after the kid legally, but she was still struggling with the best course of action. Usually open with everyone, she had shared her humiliation only with her family and a very few of her closest friends.

The jury was still out on how this would ultimately shape her. Certainly she was trying hard to bounce back. But she came home every weekend since then and took to having a small group of friends over rather than the crowds she used to pull together for a party.

~

There was a weariness about her that he had never
seen before. She still laughed and sparkled, but there was
a hint of sadness in her smile and a wisp of doubt in her
eyes. He couldn't bear to see her that way and, as he
reached for the phone to call her again, he realized his fist
was clenched. He hadn't been able to drag it out of her
who did this to her, because, he suspected, she knew he
would kill the guy if he had the chance.

As the phone went into voicemail, he smiled a little as
he always did when he heard her silly greeting. *Hello?*
Hello? I can't hear you. Who is it? Hello? Why won't you
answer? He often fell for it, but not today. Today he was
too worried. *Emma, you had better be on your way,* he ad-
monished her, and as he hung up he met Vicki's eyes and
saw his own fear reflected there.

Vicki was the heart and soul of Town House. She was
the hostess, she cooked the soups and baked the desserts,
and she was everybody's mom. She looked so sweet and
innocent, but she cussed like a sailor when customers
couldn't hear. She would occasionally have a choice
word or two about bad tippers or constant complainers,
but she was completely non-judgmental about the staff.
She protected them like a mother duck and, though
everyone thought themselves her favorite, Ben and
Emma really were.

I don't know what to do, Ben said to Vicki, and he
couldn't keep the tremor out of his voice. *She didn't go out*
last night, so I know she's home, but she's not answering.

~

The night before was a particularly sweet one. Dad tried hard to keep things fun without Mom, but they had all been so busy since Emma got back from London that there hadn't been much family time.

As Ben and Emma were getting home from work, Sarah was getting ready for bed in London, and they managed to have a decent Skype session. Ben, Emma, and Sarah were well-practiced at keeping in touch long distance. In addition to several-times-a-day texts and several-times-a-week phone calls, they had also taken to having funny sibling posts and tags on Facebook infused with inside jokes and light-hearted teasing.

But, while Sarah was still overseas, the time difference, their busy schedules, and their reliance on a solid Wi-Fi connection on both continents made it hard to have any real sibling bonding. Last night they finally managed to get it all right, and the three of them were able to catch up. They told stories and joked with comfort and ease.

Whether it was similar genetics, shared history, or years of practice, the three of them could make each other laugh like nobody else on the planet. Their Skype session was particularly funny because of the angle of the webcam. If Ben and Emma sat normally, to Sarah they looked like giants bumping their heads on the vaulted ceiling of the family room. If they tried to look proportionately "normal," they had to kneel on the floor like gophers with only their heads visible over the desk. For some reason, this had them rolling on the ground with laughter.

After their animated conversation with Sarah, Dad ordered a pizza, and they all just kind of hung out enjoying precious, relaxing time together. Over dinner,

Ben and Emma talked about art school and her new
apartment and he told her how proud he was of her.
Thannkkks, she said in that cute little way she had of
drawing it out. And he could tell that she was feeling
pretty mellow.

Paige, one of Emma's best friends came over and tried
on Emma's London outfits because she was going to
New York on Saturday, and Emma's clothes were,
according to the both of them, so hot!

Ben wanted Emma to go in the hot tub but, for the first
time he could remember, she said that she was too tired
... perhaps, she speculated, she was still a little jet lagged.
Uncharacteristically, she gave him a little hug before going upstairs, and he remembered feeling optimistic that
everything was going to be just fine.

~

He couldn't put his finger on why he was so worried.
Although she had never been late, she was a bit ditzy.
She had complained all week of being tired, so perhaps
she just overslept. If the truth be known, what was nag-
ging at him was that he had awakened abruptly at 4:04
this morning and felt so uneasy that he was almost nau-
seous. He had written it off to the pizza and then tossed
and turned the rest of the night. Had he thought of
Emma at that instant? He couldn't remember, but he had
a hazy, unsettling feeling that he had.

As he hung up for the third time, he told Vicki that
they'd better tell Doug. The last thing Ben wanted was
for Emma to get in trouble, but the patio had filled and
they needed a plan. In a weirdly complimentary way,

Doug's first reaction was concern for Emma. How far she had come that no one thought for an instant that she was just being irresponsible. *Doug, if you can take counter, I can take patio,* Ben said. *But, first, I need to call my dad.*

Rod

Chapter 5

Rod's heart raced as he tried to keep to the 30 mph speed limit. The trip from his occasional office to home typically took no more than 15 minutes, but today it seemed he caught every red light and ended up behind every little old lady in Geneva.

As he drove, Rod tried to visualize what he'd find at home. *Do I want her car to be in the driveway?* he wondered. He couldn't for the life of him remember whether he had seen it this morning. If her car were there, it would mean that she hadn't been lured out by friends after the family went to bed.

He checked his text messages when Ben called, and he had nothing from her saying she'd unexpectedly decided to spend the night somewhere. If her car weren't there, he would have no idea where to start looking for her. She knew tons of people – it was a small town and she spent her whole life there – so it seemed that every one of her friends was her best friend and at any point in time she could be with any of them.

~

Emma was a social butterfly, no question about it. But it seemed to him that she had become much more grounded in the last several weeks. Partly, he surmised, this was the result of her acceptance into art school, partly it was her trip to London. There was no doubt she walked off that plane a changed person and, though he dreaded the day coming way too fast that she would leave home and take her shining light with her, he couldn't help feeling proud that she seemed to be finding her path to becoming.

Just a few short weeks ago, they went together to rent her very first apartment. ISU had a policy that you had to stay in dorms through sophomore year and she was already denied an exception even after she tried every rationale under the sun – *I can't eat dorm food, I'm claustrophobic, I'm allergic to roommates!* But they must have over-accepted students this year because Emma unexpectedly received confirmation that she could live off campus after all if she wanted to.

By the time she received her letter, all of her friends had made other arrangements so, if she wanted to live off campus, she would have to do so alone. She considered it for all of about five minutes before the thrill of securing her very first apartment led her into his study to beg him to come with her to scope them out. Characteristically, he put everything aside, and they traveled to Bloomington the very next day. After looking carefully at several one-bedrooms, they put a deposit down on what would undoubtedly become the center of the ISU universe once Emma got there in the fall.

She was beyond excited and facetimed Mom the very instant she laid claim to her first apartment. Despite the fact that it was 1:00 in the morning in London, Mom was appropriately enthusiastic, and together they planned color schemes (red and black), the furniture they'd buy (a love seat and a Mommy-Emma chair), and how they might sneak in Juice or at least a gerbil. (The guy said no "fun" pets, and she was pretty sure she could convince him that neither Juice nor a gerbil was all that much fun!)

They started to collect items for her big move, and the dining room table was overflowing with treasures, including two spectacular finds from London – a painting of the London Tower bridge for over her bed and a lithograph of Marilyn Monroe for her bathroom. Although Dad had trouble conceiving of his youngest child being an apartment dweller, he couldn't help but get caught up in her blossoming plans for growing up.

~

Sneaking out in the middle of the night would be a definite step backwards so, yes, he decided, he definitely wanted to see her car in the driveway. And as he crossed the railroad tracks and the house came within sight, he did see it, parked right where she left it the night before. However, now that it was within view, he realized that there were all kinds of things that her still being at the house could mean, and none of them served to slow his heart rate or ease the tightness in his throat.

Almost to overcompensate, he slowed his actions way, way down. He deliberately got out of his car and locked the door. He paused to greet Monty, who had recently become so deaf that he didn't hear normal comings and goings. He glanced over at the kitchen counter and saw that the half grapefruit he left for her was still there. He didn't run up the stairs, but took them one at a time, listening intensely to see if he could hear the shower running or music coming from her room.

As he walked down the hall to her room, he observed that it was very dark, and he took a deep breath before he turned into the doorway ...

... she was there. Though the curtains hadn't been opened, he could definitely make out her shape. She was lying on her side with one leg thrown across the covers. It had been a long time since he had awakened her. She was far too grown up to stand for him singing her awake – a ritual that was their special way of greeting each day and each other until she claimed to be too old for that kind of thing and even then she indulged him for a time. *When did that end?* he found himself wondering, as he gently called her name and went to open the curtains.

Despite the sweltering July heat, her room was ice cold. Despite the midday sun, everything seemed gray and unnaturally shadowed. The pictures of her friends that covered every square inch of her walls seemed garish and taunting, and the absence of Juice was ominous.

Emma sweetie, wake up, and this time he spoke a little louder and shook her leg a little bit. Willing himself not to panic, he sat down next to her on the bed. He marveled at her beauty and, though he sensed that he should be kicking into some kind of action, he felt himself stilled by the enormity of what the next few minutes might hold.

Rarely does one stand on the precipice of something against which everything might be measured by what had come before and what would come after, and he recognized that this could be such a moment. If he sat there absorbed in her essence and took no action, would time stop and the outside world – the world where Ben was

scared and Donna and Sarah were oblivious and somewhere Emma's apartment waited for her – simply cease
to exist? If he did nothing, could he bargain with God to
switch places, to have her standing over his stillness
wondering what to do next?

Emma, he whispered and he took her in his arms and
focused all of his senses on finding a heartbeat or feeling
a wisp of breath. She seemed warm to his touch but, try
as he might, he could not feel any sense of her presence.
He cradled her against his chest and breathed in the little
girl smell of her hair. Despite the pricey perfume she had
recently started to wear, the soft, clean smell of her hair
was more beautiful to him, because it was one of the
things that made her Emma.

Sweetie, wake up, he pleaded and he held her away
from him slightly to see if her eye lashes fluttered or if
her parted lips formed into the soft sweet smile that
would indicate she was slowly coming back from wherever she had been. But she just lay there, and the only
thing that emanated from her was a profound stillness
that he could almost take for peacefulness. He gathered
her to his chest again and uttered sounds with such deep
meaning that even he could not be sure what he was
trying to say.

While he held her tight, he realized he had reached for
the phone and, using every ounce of strength he still pos-
sessed, he took a deep breath and dialed 911.

Emma

Chapter 6

The drive to Town House had been a weird one, no doubt about it. Emma realized that she had a lot on her mind between her amazement at finding Duck and her concern about being late. Still, she couldn't remember one second of the drive – it was as though the car found its own way.

Thank goodness, she sighed as she found plenty of parking spots. Even if she was late, it didn't look like it was crowded yet. Maybe she could just kind of sneak in. Vicki was manager today, and Vicki loved her. She would make a show of being mad about Emma being late, but as long as they weren't crowded yet, all would be forgiven within minutes.

As Emma hurried across the street, she found that she could already smell the tantalizing fragrance of cream of tomato corn soup. *Wow,* she thought. *Finding Duck and my favorite soup? It truly is my lucky day.*

As she entered the restaurant, she was a little taken aback. There were so many old people. Normally this wouldn't have given her pause. Town House did not generally attract the younger crowd, although she and Ben had talked it up enough that many of their friends became regulars. Still, it was a classic tea house, open only from 10:00 to 4:00 and, aside from the occasional group of businessmen, mostly it was a gathering place for middle-aged+ women who were willing to give up on

their diets for the day so that they could linger over the
Town House signature sandwiches and the aforementioned heavenly soups on their way to desserts that were
quite simply to die for.

No, she expected the customers to be on the old side.
What startled her was that everyone looked old, even the
servers, none of whom she recognized. *Where is everyone?*
she wondered out loud. She went out onto the patio and,
though it was filled with people, everyone seemed to be
happily served by some guy even older than Dad who
was just setting down two steaming bowls of soup at one
of her tables.

Excuse me. Who are you? she asked sweetly and he
answered, a bit rudely she thought, since this was her
section, *Elmer, who are you?*

I'm Emma, she responded, *Emma Mebane. I'm Ben's
sister.*

Who's Ben? Elmer asked.

Not wanting to diminish her perfectly contented
mood, Emma decided to leave Elmer to his (or rather her)
business and find Ben herself. She went to the counter,
knowing that Ben had early counter shift on Fridays and
so would be busy making drinks and preparing desserts.
But there was some old guy behind the counter as well.
What in the world was happening?

I need to find Doug, she thought. *He'll be able to tell me
what's going on.*

She absolutely adored Doug in the special way that
one adores a first boss who is kind but firm, friendly but
removed, and super cute but gay. She worked hard to be

worthy of his respect and, as she searched for him in the kitchen, which was also filled with strangers, and as her worry that she had done something horribly wrong increased, she reflected on the one and only time she royally screwed up.

~

She had been out very late the night before, and she honestly thought someone must have slipped something into her drink, because after about 9:00 she had no awareness at all until her dad stood over her shaking her leg and telling her that she had to get up for work. She realized through a haze and a throbbing headache that she was in a lawn chair in the middle of the kitchen. (She later learned that Mom and Dad could not get her upstairs to her own bed because she had been such a dead weight.)

As she stumbled up to go to her room, Mom said, *Oh, no you don't. You need to go to work.* Emma tried everything to convince her that this was not the right course of action but, since she was having trouble connecting her brain to her mouth, Mom remained unmoved. *You have an obligation to your work, and you simply must fulfill it,* Mom insisted.

Apparently (these details were filled in later), Mom called and alerted Vicki that Emma would not be herself, and instant arrangements were made to have her shift switched to assisting – a job that involved the least contact with customers.

Mom also decided that Emma would likely be unable to physically perform her duties given that she was unable to stand up with any kind of convincing consistency.

So, the idea was hatched that Mom would go, too, and she would execute Emma's directions, and together the two of them had a small chance of pulling it off.

They didn't. Doug and Vicki sent them both home after about 20 minutes of utter confusion and a comedy of errors that generated howls of laughter when reflected on later but, up to that point, it was the longest 20 minutes in Emma's life. Doug "requested" that she meet with him the following day at 8:00 and, after sleeping off whatever that was, she spent a sleepless night anticipating that she would lose her job.

She didn't. But that conversation was burned into her head and the resultant second chance would have a special place in her heart forever.

~

He must be in the bookstore, she decided. *At the very least, maybe I'll find David.* David was Doug's partner, both in business and in life, and he owned and managed the bookstore. At one time, Emma had mistaken David's quiet demeanor for a lack of approachability. But, after she had gotten to know him, she realized he was just kind of shy. In his own way, he was just as awesome as Doug, and she was proud that he had come to care about her as much as Doug did.

She turned the corner ... and stopped in her tracks. The books had disappeared and in their place were rows and rows of the most breathtaking purses she had ever seen (Juicy Couture, Prada, and Coach). But that's not all. There were Jimmy Choo shoes and Gucci dresses and

Tiffany jewelry. There were Ugg boots and Victoria's
Secret bras and Burberry coats.

The bookstore was designed for maximum nook-and-
cranniness, and customers often commented that it
seemed to go on and on. Try as she might, Emma had
never fully appreciated how special it was. Books were
not her thing, and old books were definitely not, and
books in quantity actually made her nervous. But this?
OMG. Every spot was taken with something fashionable
and totally cool, and Emma would have saved for
months to buy any single item and done so happily. She
could not have conjured up something more perfect if
she had been asked to design her ideal store.

As she stood there trying to soak it all in, she became
aware that there was another person in the room standing behind her. She turned toward the presence she
sensed, half expecting that at long last she found Doug.
But it wasn't Doug. It looked like her great Aunt Pat who
had died unexpectedly after a routine procedure in
November. It looked like her, and yet it didn't.

~

Aunt Pat was Grandma's only sister, and Mom always
talked about how gorgeous she had been when she was
younger. She always seemed old to Emma, but she was
kind of hip for an old person. She was always impeccably
dressed, wore jewelry that Emma actually envied, and
had a perfect figure. Best of all, you could always count
on her for a good shop.

For many years, Emma and her family made the long
trek to the East Coast to spend Thanksgiving with Aunt

Pat and Grandma, and on Black Friday, when most of the cousins and parents were planted in front of the TV eating leftover turkey, Aunt Pat would signal Emma and they would slip out and hit the malls.

Together they would explore all the bargains, and Aunt Pat always let Emma pick out one special treat and buy it for her. The main criterion was that it be something Mom wouldn't get for her (lipstick at age 8, for example, or fishnet hose at age 13). This shared secret and hint of naughtiness always made the purchase all the more special.

~

Maybe I'm thinking about Aunt Pat because this would be her idea of heaven, Emma reflected. Although this person looked like Aunt Pat, she had a glow about her that was hard to look away from, and Emma almost involuntarily started across the aisle towards her. As she drew closer, Aunt Pat smiled and nodded and held out her arms. *Emma, darling,* she said, *I think you need a hug,* and Emma was suddenly very, very afraid.

No, she whimpered. *No. No. No. This can't be. Please, please. I love my life. It's simply not possible. I can't be ... Please, dear God or whoever can make this go away. Make this go away. I cannot be here. This cannot be. I'm healthy and strong and I'm only 19 years old. I have a mom and a dad and a sister and two brothers and a cat and an apartment, and I'm going to be an artist.*

Emma closed her eyes and felt a nearly debilitating sense of loss and disorientation. She started to weep and, as the tears spilled down her cheeks, she focused all of her energy on thoughts of her dad. Her dad would know what to do. Her dad always knew what to do. Like he said, he was on her team. He was always on her team ... *He will fix this. He will make it right.*

Dad, she cried. *Dad, please, please find me.*

Community

Chapter 7

Is she okay? Is she going to live?

Please sir, we're doing all we can. You need to stay in your room and let the medics work.

But she's alive, right? Can you just tell me that? She's still alive, right?

The medics are doing what they can, sir. You can help best by staying out of their way.

⟩⟩⟩⟩

Where are you taking her? Is she going to live?

We've done what we can. We're transporting her to the hospital. They're better equipped there.

But is she breathing? That's why you have the tubes in her, right? Can I stay with her? Should I go in the ambulance? She'll be scared. Can I see her?

It would be best for you to follow us.

⟩⟩⟩⟩

Ben, you should come to the hospital as soon as possible.

Is she going to be okay?

It looks bad. I'm just not sure. Please come as soon as you can. Can you drive? Can someone bring you? Do you want me to come get you?

I'm okay. You stay with Emma. She needs you. I'll be okay. I'll be there soon. Tell her I love her.

⟩⟩⟩⟩

Pray for my sister.

>>>>

Hello, is this Jake? This is Officer Dean. I'd like to ask you a couple of questions about Emma Mebane. Her father tells us that she may have been at your house last night ... She wasn't? Wasn't there a party at your house last night? ... Are you sure it was Wednesday? Is there someone who can confirm that? ... I'm not able to tell you why, except that we're trying to reconstruct her recent activities. You've been helpful. Thank you.

>>>>

Paige, it's Teague. The police are here. Can you come home? They want to talk with you about Emma ... I don't know, just come home.

>>>>

Hello, Paige. My name is Officer Dean. We need to ask you a few questions about Emma Mebane. Let's sit down over here.

What's wrong – is everything okay? Is Emma okay?

We understand that you spent some time with her last night. Did anything unusual happen?

No, why?

We just need to know what happened last night. How was Emma when you saw her?

She was great. We tried on clothes. We laughed. I wanted her to go out, but she was tired and wanted to go to bed.

So she didn't go to a party at Jake's?

No, a few of us including Emma, spent a little time at Jake's the night before. But not last night.

*So she seemed okay to you last night? She didn't seem
depressed or sick or anything.*

> No. Please. You're scaring me. Emma seemed like
> Emma. She was so happy for me because I was go-
> ing to Fashion Week in New York. She lent me
> some clothes. We had a lot of fun. We hugged. I left
> and she went to bed. What's wrong? Is she okay?
> She's my best friend. What's happening?

*I'm afraid she's in the hospital and we're trying to figure out
the sequence of events.*

> (PAIGE CRYING) What do you mean she's in the hos-
> pital? Is she going to be okay? I just saw her. She
> was fine. What do you mean she's in the hospital?
> What's going on?

I can't really say anything else. I'm sorry.

$>>>>$

*Emma, call me immediately when you get this. The police
talked to me and Paige, too. What's happening? Call me. Love
you. It's Carrie. But you know that, baby girl. You're kind of
scaring us.*

$>>>>$

*Kevin, it's Paige. Did the police talk with you about Emma?
Yeah, they came to my house ... You too? What did they say?
Yeah, that's pretty much what they said to me too ... I'm calling Rodney. I hope everything's okay ... I'm kind of worried,
too. Don't you panic 'cause that would totally freak me out.
This is Emma we're talking about. She's probably fine. She
always is!*

$>>>>$

Ben, what's going on? Where's Emma? Is she okay?

〉〉〉〉

I think we should go to the hospital. I'm guessing Mr. Mebane is there with her. Maybe we can see her or at least talk to him.

〉〉〉〉

Mr. Mebane. There are three kids out front asking to see Emma. Do you want to talk with them? ... That's fine. I'll take care of it.

〉〉〉〉

112 entries on Facebook ...

 Where's Emma ...

Emma, what's going on ...

Are you okay? ...

I heard she was in the hospital ...

I heard it was bad ...

I heard she died ...

Shut up ... Don't even think such a thing. She'll be
   fine ...

Did you see her? ...

Where is she? ...

Oh my god ...

〉〉〉〉

Rodney, it's Paige. The police came to see me and Kevin and Carrie, too. What's going on? We're trying to get ahold of Em. We tried to see her and they wouldn't let us. Is she okay? Can you call me? Please tell Emma we all love her and we are praying for her. Is there anything we can do? We all want to help. We love you. Can you call as soon as you can?

~

Sarah, it's Dad. You need to call me back as soon as you get this message. It's important.

>>>>

Dad, what's up? Mom's at the hotel. I'm walking back from my bike ride. What's going on?

>>>>

Hi, sweetie, how was your bike tour?

What's wrong? Why are you crying? Who's on the phone?

>>>>

It's me. The worst possible thing has happened ...

> No, no, no, no, no, no, no, NOOOOOOOO, NOOOOOOOOOO. NOOOOOOO ... That's not possible ... She's our baby ... That can't be ... There must be some mistake ... Wait ... This doesn't happen in our family ... Wait ... Don't say it ... Wait ... I need to get there. Don't say it. It can't be. There's been a mistake ... We can figure this out ... No, this can't have happened. There's a mistake. I'll be there tonight ... Don't say this ... I'll be there ...

>>>>

We need to make arrangements to leave Amsterdam immedi-ately. There are two of us. My daughter and I. We need to get home right away.

 〉〉〉〉

Mom, you should try to get some rest.

 〉〉〉〉

There are 4652 miles left. 4651, 4650, 4649 ...

 〉〉〉〉

Mom, can you close your eyes for a few minutes and rest?

 〉〉〉〉

There are 3091, 3090, 3089 miles to go.

 〉〉〉〉

This cannot be real. There's been a terrible mistake.

 〉〉〉〉

965, 964, 963, 962 ...

~

Is Emma okay?

> No, Paige, I'm afraid she's not okay. I need for you to do me a favor ... I need for you to get a message out to Emma's friends.

Emma / Rod

Chapter 8

Emma opened her eyes, and there he was. Her dad. *Thank God.* He was sitting with his back to her in some kind of sterile looking room. She tried to run to him, but she couldn't seem to make her legs work right. And there seemed to be some kind of invisible barrier or force field or something between them.

Dad, what's going on?

Oh, Emma. Where are you? Where have you gone?

Dad, I'm right here. Turn around Dad. I'm okay. I was in some kind of weird place, or else I was having a bad dream or something. Again, she tried to go to him, but was blocked.

I keep thinking about the other times we sat here. There was the time you broke your wrist and the time you fell and hurt your ankle and the time you hit your head and had a concussion and the two times you had too much to drink. You lay there, this same way. Your eyes were closed and you looked so lovely. We always worried so much about you. You're our baby. I think you always worry the most about the baby. We worked so hard to keep you safe.

Daddy, I didn't mean to make you worry all those times. I love you. I'm here.

Oh, baby, open your eyes. Come back to me. I won't be able to bear life without you. It's so dark. I need your shine. We all do. Your mom and Sarah are coming. They're on their way. I don't know if I can face their pain. Emma, please come back.

Wait, what? Why are Mom and Sarah coming back from Amsterdam? Dad, I don't know what happened, but this is no big deal. I'm here. Aw, Dad, don't cry. Dad, please.

Emma started to feel confused and scared again. She was a girl whom it was hard to rattle. She had dealt with her fair share of disappointments, but she always found a way to go with the flow. But this had been a long day, and she was on the brink of losing it.

A nurse came in the room. Startled, Emma turned sharply and the barrier shifted slightly. Intrigued, Emma put both hands out and side stepped. The "glass" shifted again. She realized that with a certain motion she could change the angle of what she could see. It was almost like a full body version of changing her iPod screen with her fingers.

Do I need to go? Rod asked.

No. You can stay with her for as long as you want. I just wanted to see if I could get you anything?

I don't want her to be alone. I'll stay until they take her to the funeral home.

And with a final thrust of the barrier, Emma came face to face with her dad who was sitting next to her body, stroking her hair, holding her hand and crying in a way she had never seen him cry.

Emma stood very still. She felt a profound sadness. It was like she was falling through a dark tunnel that she instinctively knew had no end. All of the times she had been sad – when Duck, and Grandpa Mebane and Nanna and Grandaddy and Aunt Pat died ... every time she watched *The Notebook* and every sad story she ever heard

... every time she missed her family and every time she felt alone ... every time she'd felt failure and every fight she'd had with a friend – all of these experiences merged and multiplied and she was adrift in an endless sea of grief.

She lost herself to despair so overwhelming that she may have stopped breathing. She drifted deeper and deeper into darkness, trying desperately to find her way toward any ray of light, but there were none. She tried for what seemed hours to find a hold that might keep her from washing away into nothing.

As she stood helpless against the crushing weight on her chest, she began to become aware of other points of sorrow making their way into her consciousness ... the death of pets she had never known, the miscarriages of two babies she suddenly knew as sisters but about whom she had previously been oblivious, the heartbreak of losing a job and the fear that the family would suffer because of it.

Slowly, she became aware that this grief was not just her own ... that she was connecting with her dad on a level she had never experienced. And, as she recognized that her grief was his grief, the wall that separated them fell away, and she reached out and touched him.

Eventually, a new sea of feeling began to engulf her, and its gently lapping waves of light and warmth began to carry the darkness and sadness away. She felt infused with a sense of peace and a vast sense of knowing. She knew her father completely and utterly. She saw him as a child, then as a young man, all full of vigor and endless confidence. She experienced his love of life and under-stood his quirkiness.

She felt his love for her stripped to its bare essence. Gone was the layer that worried for her and fathered her by enforcing the rules of growing up and setting pa-rameters for behaving. What was left was the pure joy of loving her, and she opened herself up to this and felt it wash over her and strengthen her. She felt ready to ex-perience what lay ahead ... in fact she began to feel almost drawn to it.

It's going to be okay, Dad, I promise you. I'm here and I love you and we're going to be just fine.

As she leaned in to hug him, he reached out and touched her hand where it lay on his shoulder. *I love you, too,* he whispered. *I will always be on your team, no matter what you do, no matter where you are. Be well, my angel.*

Emma smiled and gave into the building force that was pulling her toward something she no longer feared.

Emma

Chapter 9

Emma couldn't see her dad anymore, which she instinctively understood was a good thing ... at least for the moment. But she couldn't see anything else either. She found herself enveloped in mist that, though not unpleasant, was definitely inconvenient. She felt a little thrill of excitement, but she couldn't for the life of her figure out quite what to do next.

She found that thinking wasn't doing much for her, so she closed her eyes and gave in to her feelings. She was feeling like she definitely wanted to check out the Town House turned-most-awesome-bookstore-ever again, and she kind of wanted to get that hug from poor Aunt Pat whom she definitely left in a most unconventional fashion when she transported (or whatever that was) to the hospital.

She gave into those wants and they started to build into real desire, and finally she felt herself sway a little and she began to have a sensation of movement. She wanted to open her eyes but wasn't sure what was making what happen, so she kept them closed until all the sensations she was feeling stilled.

She opened her eyes and – *OMG* – there she was back among the Coach purses, and there was Aunt Pat grinning from ear to ear and still all glowy and sparkly and looking altogether like the most beautiful sight she had ever seen.

Emma smiled back. *I think I'll take that hug now,* she said, and Aunt Pat enveloped her in her arms, and she sighed with joy as she was drawn into Aunt Pat's inner core of utter peace and gentle wisdom. They stood like that for a few minutes until Aunt Pat broke the silence.

Well, let's shop, she said, and starting rubbing her nose as she always did when she was particularly intense about something of interest.

Do I need money? asked Emma.

Hell, no, said Aunt Pat. *What fun would that be? Do you know the price of some of this stuff?*

They spent what could have been days putting together the most flattering outfits, with absolutely perfect accessories.

Though Aunt Pat had always been one of her favorite relatives, over the course of the afternoon her love for Aunt Pat *(call me Patsy,* she said at one point, *your mom always did)* grew and grew until she found herself wondering why she hadn't spent more time with her before now. By the end of their shop, she felt like she was her Aunt and her friend and her stylist and her confidant all rolled into one.

Let's treat ourselves, Emma said. *You are going to love the food here.*

They parked their packages and went into the restaurant and were taken to the best table in the place. They were served by Elmer, who was decidedly nicer to her now that she was a customer and not trying to steal his section.

As they savored the tomato corn soup and threw caution to the wind and ordered one each of every dessert, Emma finally turned the conversation to the questions that were increasingly on her mind.

What is this place? Is it heaven? She asked.

I'm not really sure, Patsy replied. *I don't really think about it all that much. From what I can make out, it is sort of what you want it to be.*

Do you live in Geneva now? Emma asked.

Not exactly. And I'm not exactly sure how I got here. I was watching over my great grandbabies and suddenly I was here. I must admit, I was a little shocked when I realized that I was here to greet you of all people. I knew I'd see you someday, but I certainly didn't think it would be anytime soon.

How did I ... I mean, I'm only 19. I was tired, but I didn't feel sick or anything. Why ... Emma trailed off, not quite sure how to ask what she most wanted to know.

Again, the gentle and beatific smile. *I don't know, sweetie. Sometimes, it's just your time. Who knows why I'm here instead of your grandmother who has been so sick? Who knows why you made it through all of those crazy stunts you pulled when you were younger – now, now, now. Don't protest.*

I know there were times when you shouldn't have gotten in the car with someone or had just a wee bit too much to drink or were nice to someone you didn't really know even though he set off warning signals in your head. Why were you okay through all of that and then came here one early morning when all you did was go to sleep in your own bed, in your own room, with your own cat by your side?

She reached out to brush aside a piece of Emma's lovely hair. *I just don't know,* she said again and she smiled gently. *But what I do know is that it really doesn't matter in the grand scheme of things.*

Emma thought about this for a few minutes and found that she wasn't sad exactly. Mostly she felt curious, and she continued to have a strong sense of calm mixed with hints of excitement for what the future would hold. Still, she knew that her family would be absolutely freaking out.

What happens now? Will I ever see my family again? Where will I live? What will I do?

Whoa, whoa, said Aunt Pat. *A lot of this you're going to have to figure out for yourself. I will tell you that you will learn to love it here. It's certainly different but it's every bit as special as the life you had. But you are going to have to figure some stuff out for yourself. I'm not 100% sure, but I think it may be different for each person. I've only been here since November myself, so I certainly don't have all the answers.*

But will I see my family again? Emma persisted, and she could feel little bubbles of sadness start to threaten her calm.

Absolutely, Aunt Pat assured her. *I can see whomever I want whenever I want. But, sometimes I can only see them from a great distance, and I don't think they can see me,* she sighed as a hint of wistfulness started to creep into her voice. *But,* she said as she shook her head and visibly started to glow again. *There's plenty of time for you to work all that out. For now, let's get you settled in.*

Settled in where? Emma asked.

Why, 1616 Forest Lane, of course. It's where you've lived your whole life.

Are you coming, too? Emma asked.

Of course, Aunt Pat exclaimed. *I'm going to take care of you while you get used to things.*

Emma wasn't sure quite how she felt about that. She totally had a blast with *Patsy* today. But she was 19, almost 20, and she wasn't sure that she wanted her style cramped by having a guardian hovering over her.

As if she read her thoughts, Aunt Pat smiled again. *Listen, honey. I have my own life. I was pretty content watching Kaylee trying to take her first steps when I got an overpowering feeling that I needed to be here and suddenly I was. I don't think I'm meant to stay here. I think I just need to help you get settled in and then we'll see.*

That sounded reasonable and like the kind of plan that Emma liked best – a few next steps worked out, but mixed with a heavy dose of what-will-be-will-be. Even though she didn't have to pay, she did leave a tip for Elmer (the old fuddy duddy didn't deserve it, but it made her happy), stood up and closed her eyes and started swaying a little.

What in the world are you doing? chuckled Aunt Pat.

I'm trying to beam us home ... Emma said a little uncertainly.

Patsy laughed and grabbed her hand. *Let's take your car. It'll be way, way easier,* she said and, as they walked toward the parking lot, she whistled and a gorgeous golden retriever, who had clearly been waiting patiently under the bench for them, leapt over to her side. *You re-*

member Honey, don't you? she asked and, though Emma didn't exactly, she pretended she did and bent down to pat Honey's lovely head and scratch her ears. *Won't Duck love you?* she cooed, and she felt back in touch with her inner peace.

On the drive home, Emma paid a little more attention than she did on the way to work. *Geneva was the same, but better,* she decided. Everything was so bright and almost lush. She always felt that Illinois was way too flat, and she especially felt this way after experiencing the rolling hills of Ireland. But as she traversed the short trip home, she almost felt that she was back in Ireland, and she half expected to see heather cropping up here and there.

Wow, Geneva really is a beautiful place to live, she thought happily and realized that she was looking forward to rediscovering it through her new-found perspective.

When they got home, Duck showed his delight at her return, then appropriately welcomed Patsy and Honey and only briefly searched for Ben before running off with Honey to introduce her to all the best parts of the house and his multiple baskets of chew toys, which he was absolutely willing to share in exchange for the company of a four-legged friend.

Are you tired at all, snookums? asked Patsy, and Emma realized that she wasn't the least bit, though she knew she should be.

Not really, she said, and Aunt Pat explained that, in her case, she did sometimes sleep, but it was more from the pleasure of closing her eyes and taking a break from her experiences than because she was tired.

I'm going to do that now, she said. *I think I'll go up to your mom and dad's room.* But, when she saw the look of horror on Emma's face, she correctly surmised that Emma wouldn't want her taking over her parents' room. *Come to think of it,* she said quickly, *I think I'd rather set up in the guest room.*

Emma was alone again, and she welcomed it. Her head was spinning and, although it wasn't tiring, she did find that she had to be deliberate about staying connected to her happiness rather than let sadness seep in.

She realized with a start that she hadn't thought about what was happening with her family the whole afternoon. *Does that make me a bad person?* she wondered, and decided that she needed to do what felt right to do. It seemed to be the only road map she had, and so far it served her well.

She settled herself into her favorite spot on the couch and watched a few reruns of *Vampire Diaries* (from the first season, before you realize quite how hot Damon is and how much better a match he is for Elana than boring Stefan), just to clear her brain.

Time passed, but Emma didn't have a clear sense of how much time and, though she thought vaguely that it should probably be dark, there seemed to be a constancy to the weather that was, well, perfect.

She thought about how much Ben wanted to move back to San Diego and realized that Geneva felt an awful lot like Southern California at the moment. Though it was sweltering "yesterday," it was decidedly milder today and nowhere near as muggy.

She checked her iPhone just to see if she could get a sense of timing and realized that it was still blinking 4:04, so it was apparently pretty useless. Idly, she started to play around with other features of the phone. *I'm not sure how I will live without my phone*, she thought but, then again, she suddenly realized that she had no one to call.

Like before, little speckles of wistfulness started to sweep over her, and she clicked on Facebook, just to see if she still had pictures of all of her friends.

 I love you Emma. Every time I saw you, you made me laugh. You are such a caring and loving person, you always made me feel so happy. I'm going to miss you love. Rest in peace.

 You are an amazing person Emma. We had so many great times and you were such a good friend to me no matter what. I love you and am going to miss you so much. You will always be my best friend and I will hold you in my heart forever.

 I love you Emmers

Wait, what?????

 I miss you so much mebs.

 We had so much to look forward to, Emma. You will be missed dearly. I love you so much.

Emma was almost afraid to breathe. She flipped back to her Wall and saw that there were 211 unread notifications. Was this possible? Could she still read her Wall posts?

You were my first and best friend in Geneva and always will be. I love you!

I am stunned. I wish more than anything that the bad news I just heard wasn't true. You were such an amazing, vibrant, funny and beautiful girl. I can't imagine coming home and not seeing your sunny smile.

Emma, I am still in disbelief that this happened. I just want to remind you of how your life blessed mine. It all started back in 7th grade when you came to all of my home baseball games. You would always sit on the bleachers with your army of friends. Somewhere along the way you found out that you had seen me before. As it turns out, I was that home-schooled kid who defied the rules of normalcy and was on the middle school boys basketball team and the traveling baseball team. DeLaBar officially introduced me to you the following summer. Now we were almost in high school and the big rumor was that this Max kid, me, was going to GHS. I was stressed, excited, concerned, and a whole host of other emotions were present. My very first day of public school, you made the decision that you were going to help me out. I was a full 8 years behind on the public school thing. That day, despite being in a school full of people you knew, you chose to hang with me in all classes we had together. Over the next few months, you taught me how to navigate the public school life. You answered my hundreds of questions I had − about teachers, homework, other classmates of ours. You introduced me to all your friends and reintroduced me again, as I was quite overwhelmed with learning the names and faces of hundreds of new people. You even told me the names of girls you knew who had secret crushes on me. Emma, without you in my life, I honestly do not know how my time at GHS would have turned out. You got me started on a strong foothold. Aside from the few people I knew already, you were the first person to befriend me. I will remember you always, every single day of my life.

Awwww, thought Emma, as she read pages and pages of friends pouring out their hearts to her. It seemed that, just as she read one, two or three more would pop up. On and on she read, and she was overwhelmed with the pure love that she felt emanating from the page after page of entries.

There was Carrie *(aw, Carrie, don't cry baby love. I'm here)*

and Kevin *(Kevin, don't lose it. Hang in there, I'm fine, don't worry)*

and Paige *(Paige, be tough. Don't fall apart. You couldn't have done anything that night)*

and friends from high school, and from soccer, and from ISU, and friends she hadn't spoken to in months ...

There were friends of her sister and her brother and her mom ...

She realized that every profile picture had been changed to include a picture of her. Dozens and dozens of pictures of her smiling face, people kissing her and laughing with her and hugging her ...

Poems – *(aw, Zack, I love you, too. Why the heck didn't we ever go out??)*

and songs and quotes

and everyone was trying to express what a dark place their world would be without her.

The world lost a bright ray of sunshine ...

You are loved by so many ...

I won't be truly happy until I see your sweet face again ...

You changed all of our lives for the better ...

Your beautiful smile and your infectious laugh are gone forever but will never, ever be forgotten ...

How will we survive in a world without you ...

I feel so sorry for anyone who has not yet met you and loved you, they will never be blessed with having you in their world ...

A part of me is gone with you and a part of you will always be with me ...

It was hard to understand what she was feeling because the feelings were so strong, conflicting, and complex. It wasn't happy exactly, because she missed her friends desperately. But she felt intimately connected to the whole world of all the people she had ever known.

She could feel a deep, deep well of love and understood that the energy that spilled off the screen was generated by connection to her – she stood in the middle of everything that was said and every entry that was liked and every comment and every tag and every picture. She felt warm and cozy all over, and she felt kind of proud even though she felt weirded out about any kind of positive feelings that came from the pain of others.

She touched the pictures of each of her friends and called to Duck to be with her so that she could feel the warmth of another living thing while she read and read and read ...

After what could have been hours, she saw her sister's picture, and she paused because she wasn't sure she was quite ready to read what she said. She stood and stretched and thought to wake up Aunt Pat so she could get something to eat but, when she realized she wasn't

hungry, she snuggled up with Duck again, took a deep
breath, and readied herself.

My family has been so touched by the support, the
stories, and the love of Emma that you have all
shared with us and with each other. We know that you
are struggling, as we are, to make any kind of sense
of what has happened. Please continue to celebrate
Emma's life though memories of her. They bring us
comfort in this, our darkest hour.

... and a little later, from Ben ...

Please join Emma's family in a visitation service to
celebrate her life today, starting at 4:00. Emma's
funeral will be held tomorrow the 14th at 11:00. Follow
this link for details and location information.

Emma sat holding her phone to her heart, along with
the pictures of Ben and Sarah, as she tried to process everything she had seen and read.

She realized that she had likely missed the visitation,
and she was glad. She wasn't sure she was ready to connect with the suffering of her whole family, and she
knew that she would really struggle seeing her Mom for
the first time since ... well, since she'd come home from
Amsterdam.

But she decided that she wanted to go to her funeral
(*am I really thinking this thought?* she wondered, and

almost laughed at the absurdity of planning to watch her own funeral).

As she stretched again and stood up, dumping Duck off her lap, she realized that this time she really was hungry, and she went off to wake up Patsy so they could have dinner and plan for tomorrow.

What will I wear? she wondered and for some reason this thought made her laugh out loud! *How utterly bizarre,* she said to Duck, who thumped his tail in agreement and gazed adoringly up at her.

I hope the speeches for me are as good as they were for you, she said, and went into the kitchen to start setting the table.

Carol

Carol felt helpless. Usually she took charge by cleaning, but this did not seem to be what was needed. Even if it would help, she wasn't sure she had enough energy to make a difference. She busied herself by organizing and reorganizing the cards and letters that were starting to come in and by answering the phone, repeating by rote now, *No, they can't come to the phone right now ... They appreciate your thoughts and prayers very much ... No, there's nothing you can do ... Honestly, we have plenty of food ... Yes, I'll tell them you called ...*

She greatly preferred the calls that were from adults because they knew how to handle themselves with what she herself had learned over the years was appropriate pre-funeral behavior. Emma's friends, on the other hand, threw her. They were so shocked and so honest in their sadness that she felt overwhelmed all over again when one of them was on the other end of the phone. No platitudes from them. And they often just showed up at the door to sit in Emma's room for a while or to take turns in her favorite chair in the basement. Instead of cards, they brought an eclectic mix of things they thought Emma would like – a bottle of 99 Banana's (*what in the world?*), a military epaulet she had always jokingly said she wanted from one of her best friend's boyfriend's jacket, chocolate covered strawberries, a CD of her favorite songs, baskets of flowers (it seems they didn't know that sunflowers were not appropriate for death, but, then again, they were, oh, so right for Emma), and several different offerings having something to do with stars. Shining, it seemed, was something that immediately and universally became a theme when friends thought of what would be missed most about Emma's presence in their lives.

She learned about Emma from a phone call that she got while on an annual vacation to her beloved Ocean City. Unmarried herself, she was the personification of the "cool" aunt and had a unique relationship with each of the Mebane siblings and her sister Susan's daughter, Katy.

～

What she now knew was Emma's last day on earth had been a picture perfect one at the shore. She and Katy went to the beach early that day and found a choice spot to set up, exactly far enough from the water that you wouldn't have to move when it was high tide. The sun was warm and the water cool.

She remembered watching a family playing paddle ball and envied the young parents for their excited children who were just starting to turn pink. She and Katy jumped waves and executed some perfect body surfs. They relaxed on their towels for a while, she reading a book called *Sisters* and Katy working on her tan. They eventually packed it up and headed back to the cottage just as the sun was starting to wane and the air was turning slightly chilly.

That night, after dinner, Carol crawled into bed exhausted, but curiously unable to sleep. She had earlier downloaded the Jewel *Lullaby* CD, so she played it on her iPhone and tried to settle in.

As she listened to the gentle sound of Jewel's voice and the beautiful songs she sang about children sleeping and parents keeping them safe, she found her thoughts increasingly occupied by Emma. She had asked Emma to join Katy and her at the shore, but Emma couldn't get the time off since it was so soon after her London trip.

The previous year, Emma and Sarah had both vacationed with Carol in the very same house for a week. It was the first time Carol thought of Emma as an adult and one whom she wanted to get to know better. She always loved the child and relished the opportunity to get to know and love the grown-up.

Two years before, Carol agreed to chaperone Emma and two of Emma's best friends – Paige and Mel – for a week at the shore. She had no idea what she was getting herself into! Ocean City was in a dry county and Emma, of course, didn't know anyone, so Carol naively assumed that they would simply enjoy their days at the beach together and spend quiet evenings at home. That was not to be. Within 60 minutes of arriving at the house, before the beds were even made or groceries put away, several boys showed up on the front porch bearing gifts of beer, looking for all the world like they had never seen three girls their own age.

Even now, Carol wasn't quite sure how it happened, but she spent 24 hours in utter terror that they would all somehow end up in jail – and on her watch yet. She finally called Donna who had a stern talk with all three of them ending with a threat to drive all the way to the East Coast to bring them home if they didn't shape up.

Things settled down considerably after that, and Carol was actually able to enjoy living the week vicariously through their eyes. One incident she remembered with absolute clarity was watching Emma as she was returning from a swim. In all the time she and her sisters had been coming to the shore, they had never ever been ones that the lifeguards noticed. Yet, as Emma started past the lifeguard stand, one of them must have called out to her. She paused, shaded her eyes, and lifted her hand to receive, with flourish and flair, a "rose" crafted out of aluminum foil that likely had been whipped up from someone's sandwich wrapping. Emma giggled, gave a little curtsey and, with several pairs of eyes admiring her bright green bikini *and* her rose, sashayed back to their blanket. Oh, to be young and Emma!

Previous summers had always included at least a few day trips to the shore during Donna's family visits to her parents but, with Donna in London and Sarah, Ben and Emma working, this would be the first summer that didn't include time spent together. So, Carol could understand why she was feeling so nostalgic, but she was a little mystified that her thoughts kept going to Emma specifically.

> *Close your eyes,*
> *Don't ask why.*
> *Let's dream together you and I*
> *Oh, close your eyes*
> *And we'll fly*
> *Dreaming together you and I.*

She finally drifted off, but her sleep was restless.

The next day, after a leisurely morning and plenty of coffee, she and Katy decided to drive to the boardwalk for the afternoon and, just as they started, her phone went off. It was the Skype ring that signaled it was probably Donna and Sarah, calling to regale them with stories about their first day in Amsterdam. She would always remember the way she and Katy had looked at each other after the first ring. *Donna!!!* they both exclaimed, grinning with anticipation.

~

It was too soon to relive those next few minutes, and she put them down into the dark well of her grief. Someday she would have to process them again, but not today.

Today they had to figure out a place large enough to hold the crowds they knew would attend Emma's viewing and a place that would allow them to hold her funeral despite their not being church-goers. *(No, Rod, though Emma would love it, the neighbor's country club is simply <u>not</u> an option.)*

Today, they had to order food to feed her friends, and find a perfect picture of her so strangers could do her makeup, and find a dress she would want to be buried in, and remember which pillow was her absolute favorite so they could rest her head gently on it.

Today, they had to figure out how to comfort Juice who seemed to be trying to find her, and they had to write the obituary that would summarize her life and cause those who didn't know her to pause before moving on to the Sports or Entertainment sections and take a moment to wonder how a lovely 19-year-old could have died peacefully in her sleep.

Today might be the day that Donna would finally change the clothes she had been wearing since Amsterdam or Rod would stop talking nonstop or Jason would drink something other than beer.

These were the rituals of death, she knew. She was a neonatal nurse in inner city Philadelphia, and she had rocked her fair share of babies knowing that they were about to go to a better place than the one that likely awaited most of them on earth. Though she felt sad for her tiny charges, usually her pity was mixed with a sense of inner peace. She believed in God, and in a weird way sending Him babies who never really had a chance had strengthened her faith.

But the idea of sending Emma off to God was appalling. A life that large and a light that bright had no business being snuffed out after only 19 short years. She wished with all her heart that ... that what? That if she had convinced Emma to come to the shore, things might have turned out differently? That she had talked with her more, learned every possible thing there was to know about her, and somehow been more present in her life? That the God she believed in had taken her instead of sweet, funny Emma?

Feeling the unbearable weight of a thousand *what ifs*, Carol roused herself to go answer another phone call.

Community

Chapter 11

... and, Lord, that's why we are gathered here this morning — to celebrate the life of a beautiful young lady so suddenly taken from our presence ...

~

Ben tried to listen to what the minister was saying, but he was mostly lost in his own thoughts. Aside from an occasional assignment in school, he had never formally spoken in front of people, but he knew right away that it was something he simply had to do. There was no way he was going to let them take his sister away without telling the world why she was so special.

He was nervous about speaking, of course. However, he had carefully written out the exact words he wanted to say, and he was ready ... for the speech part. But what he really was regretting was his promise to the family that he would sing. Again, something he felt compelled to do, but his anxiety over screwing up increased by the moment. In a crazy kind of way, though, he was grateful to have some kind of feeling cutting through the heart-ache that has been eating him alive from the inside out.

As the pastor called his name, he stood and walked to the front of the church. He paused to look at Emma's casket, and his nervousness faded. He cleared his throat and began.

If there's anything Emma's passing has taught me, it's that no one can seem to find the right words. The overwhelming outpouring of grief and condolences we have received from people Emma has touched over the years often includes the line "what can you even say?" — a question that's inevitably followed by befuddled silence. So, how in the world I'm even supposed to begin to talk about the life and inconceivable death of my baby sister is beyond me. But for her sake (and mine), I'll give it my best shot: something she always did in earnest throughout her short life.

The most daunting challenge my family and I have had in the immediate aftermath of Emma's abrupt death has been trying to envision a future without her. It's hard enough trying to picture doing <u>anything</u> without her, much less doing <u>everything</u> without her. For those of you who know the dynamics of the Mebane family, you certainly know that to be true. And, as I attempted to prepare myself for what lies ahead, I was drawn early and often to all the reminders there will be of Emma. As you all know, in a town as community-oriented as Geneva, and in an area as closely-knit as the tri-cities, the reminders will be many and close between.

As Ben spoke about the memories that were important to him and to her many friends whom he had worked so hard to ignore, he felt strangely connected to all of the faces looking up at him. They cried when he cried and smiled at the right places, and he found himself hoping that Emma's death would not sweep these people out of his life, too.

He spoke of his love/hate relationship with Emma's cat and the constant jockeying for basement rights. He spoke of all of her favorite spots around the town where she was born and where she died. He reminded them with a smile of her keen ability to pick out hands-down, without-a-doubt the most expensive thing in the entire Geneva Commons Shopping Center. He talked of dinners at their favorite restaurants and the places like JuRin and Simply Nails, which she frequented so often that she was treated like a rock star.

He spoke of the Town House family, trying to get people to understand how important they were to her and she to them. As he was winding down, he started to lose it a little. He had held it together pretty well, he thought, but it was almost as though, once he stopped talking about her, she would really truly be gone forever … and, of course, when he stopped talking, he was going to have to start singing.

The more I thought about it, the more it became clear: everything will be a reminder of Emma. And more importantly, <u>EVERYONE</u> will be a reminder of Emma. I'm just as much a reminder of her to others as they are to me. And when you look at it that way, the task seems a little less daunting. We all have the honor and the privilege of carrying on Emma's memory and reminding people of the impact she had.

So don't fight the reminders. Instead, embrace them. And let them inspire you to work a little harder, love a little deeper, laugh a little louder, hug a little tighter, and most importantly, live a little more. Emma's life was far too short, and there is no disputing that. But she lived more in her 19 years than most people do in 90. So please help us let her be an inspiration to everyone she never got a chance to meet.

Finally, I'd like to talk directly to my family for a moment. We're in this together, you guys. And the only way we'll make up for the hole Emma has left in our family unit is to huddle up even closer in this time of unbearable grief (which is great because I sure do loooove to be touched ...). I don't know where to begin, particularly at a time when all we feel is a crushing sense of finality. This is undoubtedly the hardest Mebane Send-off we'll ever have to give. But let's do as we so often did while Emma was alive, and look to her for inspiration.

As a final tribute to Emma, I would like to sing a brief song in her honor. For as long as I can remember, Emma always thought that tattoos were the coolest thing in the entire world. So when she asked me to help her pick out a song lyric for her first real tattoo, I was actually honored. We tossed around ideas for a while, with none of them striking our fancy. And then all of a sudden, the perfect song came to my mind.

It was one of those moments where you knew it was right the second you thought of it. It's a song called "Star Star," and it was written by Glen Hansard of the Frames. Its beautiful simplicity mirrors Emma so well, and the line we settled on for her tattoo became a mantra of sorts for her. So please forgive me the amateurish nature of my musical abilities and the broken-hearted nature of my performance. I'd like to sing a song to my baby sister, Emma. The girl who taught all of us how to shine ...

~

Wow, Paige thought, as Ben's pure voice rang out. He can really sing. *Who knew?* Paige was supposed to go next and, though she was honored when Rodney and Donna asked her to speak on behalf of Emma's friends, she couldn't help feeling that the whole thing was just so surreal. Had it really been less than a week ago that she and Emma had giggled and trashed her closet looking for the perfect outfit and then hugged and promised to call the second they woke up? Was it really possible that Emma would never wake up again?

I could really be totally freaked out if I let myself, she thought, but she simply had to hold it together long enough to make Emma proud. When the pastor called her name, she touched two fingers to her lips and raised them … she guessed to heaven. *This is for you, babe,* she said to Emma silently as she took her place in the front of the church.

The other day I was reading through Emma's and my Wall on Facebook. There was one post in particular that caught my eye and really made me think. Emma wrote on my Wall saying, "We are really weird people." I smiled and agreed and read my reply, "Yeah, we are really weird. But, if you weren't weird, Emma, you wouldn't be 100% perfect."

Who knew that something said in our crazy high school years could still affect me so much today? She was perfect. Her perfect laugh, her perfect light blue eyes, her perfect advice. Her perfect way of loving each and every person in her life. For me and for many others, she was a perfect best friend.

I don't know how Emma and I became so close – we just did. One day I didn't know her at all, and the next day she was my best friend. A friendship that was just meant to be, I guess.

And Paige, as Ben had before him, went on to talk about all of her favorite and perfect times with Emma, which included shared family vacations and party trips to colleges and all the times they shared at the pool and at the mall and simply jumping with Duck on the trampoline in Emma's back yard, with Donna so worried that someone would fall, but then cranking up the tunes so they could make up jumping dance routines. She knew these were the times that would always be remembered as the very best times of their whole lives. And Paige cried when she made the simple statement that she had always thought there would be more.

Paige tried as hard as she could to capture the essence of Emma as a friend. Emma was the one who believed in you, the one who stood up for the underdog, and the one who could turn tears into laugher just by being Emma. She was the one that waiters remembered and strangers stopped to talk to and teachers were easy on because you just never knew what would come out of her mouth.

It felt important to Paige that she share with Emma's family what happened that last night and let them know how very normal it all was. It was important to her that she make sure they understood that she knew how much they had all lost.

When I was at Emma's house last Thursday night to borrow some clothes for my trip to New York, of course she offered to let me borrow clothes she hasn't even worn yet from London. We talked about London the whole time and about what an amazing trip it was. At one point, she asked me if I wanted to have this new bathing suit top she ordered online. I asked her why she wanted to give it to me. She said that, when she tried it on, the clips in the middle snapped because her boobs were too big. She was really proud of those boobs!

That night was like so many nights we hung out together. But now that night will always be my fondest memory of her. She was just so happy and so proud of me, and that just about sums her up.

She could find a reason to laugh about nothing at all. And she truly was proud of all her friends for whatever they wanted to do or be. She was one of my only friends to tell me I would be successful in life. And I took that to heart – because I know the words that Emma said were always so sincere.

And, although we have lost someone who was so perfect to all of us, she can never be completely gone. She left a piece of her with each and every one of us in this room. And that piece she left with us will make us strive to be more like her every day.

I know for me I want to be a friend to everyone just like she was to me. I know I will never find a best friend like Emma because there is nobody in the world as perfect as her. But for the rest of my life, for her, I will try to be a friend like her.

~

Doug was still in shock. He had experienced many deaths in his life, and they were always tragic, each in its own way. But little Emmers? He had just seen her. She had just danced in like she always did and teased him and sassed the cooks and charmed the customers. She had worked that day ... she had worked on Thursday and, what, gone home to die?

God, he was not going to make it through this. How do you talk about a warm, sunny, happy-go-lucky girl who lay in front of you cold and gray and quiet in a box?

But the Mebanes were a big part of the Town House family, and it was important to them that he talk about what she was like to those who worked with her. He was the only boss she would ever have, and he wanted to let everyone know that she was a good employee and that this was a part of her life about which they should be proud as well. Ben and Paige had their perspective and he had his and he knew his was important, too.

I brought Emma's picture up here so I could picture happy Emma to help me get through this.

When Emma first started working at Town House, at sixteen years of age, she was the youngest employee I'd ever hired. Last night, at Emma's wake, I had the privilege to read for the first time an essay that she wrote about Town House. In it she expressed her excitement when she spoke of her interview, exclaiming "I nailed it!" To be honest, I don't specifically remember her interview, but I do remember how delightful she was from that very first day and how her brother Ben had enthusiastically endorsed her. Ben had been an employee already for a couple of years, and at first I wasn't sure that having siblings work together was such a good idea. However, I was quickly put at ease by the way Ben took Emma under his wing and welcomed her in a new environment.

It has been a joy over these past years to see the love and support that Ben and Emma had for one another. Something like that isn't always common to see between brothers and sisters. Something special.

As you would expect, Emma quickly found her place as a beloved part of the Town House family. Her cheerful nature and solid work ethic made her an absolute pleasure to work with and a favorite with our regulars. As simple as it sounds, whenever Emma would arrive at work, it always made me feel good to see her smile, and to hear her "good morning." She just had a way about her. Funny, funny Emma.

When talking to our staff about the memories they had of Emma, it seemed that laughter was a common thread through all of them. There was always a lot of laughter whenever Emma was around. She brought out the playful side of everybody, and she was just plain fun. Earlier this week a regular recalled how he came into Town House during a slow lunch one day, when Emma was working counter. Desperate for a customer and for some company, she threw herself across the counter and cried "Come sit with me ... pllleeeaasse. Be with me!"

Yesterday, Vicki, our manager, was laughing as she reminded me how Emma would pour apple juice into a wine glass and then text me a picture of her posing like she was drinking at work. You know the pose when she puts her hand on her hip – like that. Funny Emma. There are some other memories that employees have of Emma that I will just take a few minutes to share with you now ...

Doug realized, as he was reading through the memories each employee provided, that they were all about laughing and all of the silly, daily hi-jinks that happen when a bunch of young people work together. As poign- ant as the memories were to him, he realized that most of them were about nothing at all. It was so hard to capture in words the wisps of Emma that started with a smile and moved to a giggle and ended with holding-your-sides-can't-catch-your-breath peals of laughter that emanated from the very act of being with her.

As Ben and Paige had done before him, Doug was drawn to conclude by speaking directly to the Mebane family.

> *As a representative of everyone at Town House, I wish to say to the Mebanes that we hope you know we all love you. Emma was such an important part of our family, and we will always treasure having had her in our lives. In the spring, David and I plan to plant English roses called "Lady Emma Hamilton" in the Town House Shakespeare garden. We will always remember Emma's smile, her laugh and her love of life. And when the roses bloom, we will remember our little Emma as she has always been to us, sweet and beautiful and happy ...*

~

Rod had not written down what he wanted to say because his thoughts had swirled like a tornado in his head ever since he found Emma in her bed – an experience that numbed his brain and seared his heart. But he wasn't worried or nervous. He knew that, once he started, the words would just flow. And he was determined that, once he got through, every person in the sanctuary would feel the essence of Emma and hold that essence close and carry it into the future that his lovely child would never know.

Unlike the others, I didn't write my comments down, and it has my wife very nervous ... For me, though, the big question is whether I should talk at all. I debated with myself as to whether or not I should, and then my sister, Meg, reminded me that I once I said that I would give a really big speech at Emma's wedding.

Well, unfortunately, I will never have the opportunity to send Emma and a handsome new husband off to a long and prosperous future together, but I can still help to send her off in style, and that's what I'm hoping to do ...

Then, with a nod to Emma, Rod gripped the podium and recited the beginning of a prayer ...

Now I lay me down to sleep,
I pray the Lord my soul to keep.
If I should die before I wake,
I pray the Lord my soul to take ...

He then stopped and, after a solemn silence filled the air, he continued ...

Not quite a week ago, Emma went to sleep, and she did not wake up. The Lord chose to take the soul of our baby and our sister and our cousin and our niece and our grandchild and our neighbor and our friend.

There is so much obvious sadness, and that sadness is one of the things that unites us all today. We are all suddenly dealing with the sadness of profound loss. We are all trying to understand how this could happen ... to our Emma. We are all trying to figure out what it means, and we are wondering how in the world we are going to make it through

...

Well, I'm sorry ... I don't really have any answers to give you. But, over the course of the last week, various phrases have occurred to me, and a few have stuck in my mind and they have brought some comfort. I would like to share these few little nuggets of possible comfort with you ...

One phrase that occurred to me early on was related to the concept of a crescendo. All parents want their kid's life to build and to go on and on and on ... with one crescendo that follows another and another ... Well, we now know that Emma won't have that kind of run, but – here's the phrase that occurred to me:

Emma was at the top of her crescendo.

I'm coming to believe that, in the grand scheme of things, it doesn't matter that it was nineteen years or if it was thirty-nine years or fifty-nine ... Emma packed a lot of life into her nineteen years and everything important in Emma's life was coming together magically and she went out at the top. That thought helps me ...

Another phrase that came to me early was that:

Emma died in her dreams.

Emma didn't die in her sleep – she died in her dreams ... We will never know where she was when she crossed from one world to another. But I know for sure that, when I found her lying in her bed last Friday morning, it was as if she were dreaming, with her eyes closed and her cute little mouth open just a bit, and she was utterly at peace. Thinking about that helps me, too ...

Rod paused as tears started to come. Then, again after he glanced in Emma's direction, he thanked a number of individuals by name and spoke of the honor that the family felt from the outpouring of love and support of so many people in the community. He singled out Geneva's Mayor.

When the mayor passed through the line during Emma's visitation, he mentioned that on his way home he was planning to lower the city flag in Emma's honor. And, now, when you drive past City Hall, you'll see that the Geneva flag is flying at half-mast. It's a wonderful tribute to Emma, who was a Genevan through and through.

Then, turning back to Emma, he touched on the concept of "becoming" and shared some thoughts on what Emma had become for him.

For those of us here, we can't know what we will become, because we are still in the process of becoming and we don't know how much time we have remaining. The jury is still out on what we will become.

But the jury is not out on Emma. Emma has <u>become</u>. And we can begin to judge her life in the context of becoming. So far, I've come up with two big ideas on what Emma has become to me.

One is related to Charlotte's Web. There is a word that Charlotte wrote in her web that I was trying to remember this morning. I asked Sarah what Charlotte wrote in her web, and she called back her response, "some pig." Right answer, but not the one I was looking for ... The word I was thinking of (we later googled) was "radiant."

Emma has become a person of radiant beauty.

If you look at pictures of Emma, it's startling – you can't deny the shine that Ben talked about and the flat-out beauty in Emma's smile. I don't have to be boastful – I just need to be an honest parent to say that Emma was truly beautiful – she had radiant beauty. But the beauty was not just in her appearance – it was in her heart … it was in her spirit … it was in everything she said … it was in the way she touched every person she met …

The second thing that Emma has become for me:

Emma has become a source of wisdom and inspiration.

One of the really distinctive things about Emma is that she had a very definite persona – she had a very special, identifiable character – to the point that you could often predict correctly how Emma would act and react. You could ask Emma's friends in any particular situation, "What would Emma want?" and nine out of ten of them would come up with the same answer because they all knew Emma. Emma was Emma.

(That, by the way, has become an important source of guidance to us this week when we were making decisions about all sorts of things. We'd ask, "W-W-E-W: What would Emma want?" … and that helped us sort through options.)

Now, what does that have to do with wisdom and inspiration? Well, it's all about the persona itself. To say it simply, Emma has become – and now will forever stay – an incredible person … But how do we know for sure? What's the measure for Emma's life? How do we measure this "moonbeam in our hand"?

Well, you know the right measure for Emma is <u>not</u> number of years. No matter how you count it, nineteen years falls way short of being enough …

The measure that I've come up with for Emma is related to the ruby red slippers that Emma just loved for years – getting them in successively larger sizes as she got older. It was the Wizard of Oz, in speaking to the Tin Woodman, who said, "A heart is not judged by how much you love, but by how much you are loved by others."

In my opinion, <u>that</u> is the measure of Emma. And just look around ... Emma was very well loved by others ...

There are two other phrases that I'd like to mention. One is the formula I figured out for Emma that I think applies to all of us. And the formula is:

ME + EMMA = BETTER ME

Very simply, I am better because of Emma. And I suspect many of you are as well ...

The last phrase that occurred to me that I'll mention happened last Friday night – at the end of a very long day, the day that Emma died. At last, I was home, and I was alone on the back deck. The night was cool, and a strange peace shrouded in pain and disbelief had settled in ... while I waited to get my wife and older daughter back from Europe, my older son back from Seattle, and the rest of our family back together ... The phrase that occurred to me at that time was this:

My daughter is my angel now.

In closing, let me reference last Father's Day. Generally, Father's Day comes and goes in our house with not a lot of recognition. But this year, for whatever reason, Emma outdid herself, with some very thoughtful gifts and a handmade card.

I'd like to read a short quote that Emma included on the card. I think this sums Emma up pretty well. So fitting that she gave it to me on Father's Day, just three and a half weeks ago.

Life is full of beauty, notice it.
Notice the bumble bee, the small child, and the smiling faces.
Smell the rain and feel the wind,
and live your life to the fullest potential,
and fight for your dreams.

Finally, I'd like to ask a favor of all of you and, that is: Tonight, please find a loved one ... or, better yet, find a few loved ones ... and give them an extra hug and hold them tight.

Hold them tight ... all through the night ... and keep them safe 'til the morning light.

Patsy

I was a bird?! Emma exclaimed, wrinkling her nose in distaste. *A bird!* she sighed, exasperated.

What's wrong with that? asked Aunt Pat.

I got all dressed up and I looked totally awesome, and all of a sudden I realized I was sitting in a tree ... in a tree!

But could you see everything? Could you hear? What was the funeral like?

Well, yes. Apparently, I was no ordinary bird. (Emma managed to have "bird" sound like "turd.") *I could see and hear everything. I could even smell the Portillo's Italian beef, which would have made my mouth water except my mouth was a BEAK!*

Oh, Emma. What did you think would happen? Patsy asked, not unkindly. *Did you think you would just waltz up and take a seat in the front row?*

I'm not sure what I thought. I'm trying not to think too much 'cause I feel like my head might explode. I drove up to the church and parked on the street so no one would see my car. I wasn't sure if people could see me, but I was sure that, if they did, they would freak out so I was pretty careful. I snuck around to the back of the church and peeked in a few windows. I looked in on my mom for a while and, when she got up, I knew the service was about to start. I ran to the side of the church and hid behind a tree while everyone went in. Then I couldn't figure out a way to get in myself after the doors were all closed. Fortunately, I discovered a high window and, if I stood on tip toe, I could see into the sanctuary.

Somebody named Pastor Keith was talking, and I couldn't hear him so well. But then my brother started to talk, and I forgot where I was, and suddenly I could see and hear everything so clearly. At one point, Susan looked right at me and I thought I'd better move, but just then I realized that, somewhere along the way, I turned into a bird. Which is why, I guess, I had settled in so nicely onto a tree branch. So, I could see, but I was a bird.

Stop with the bird thing, Patsy laughed. *You'd think you turned into a spider! A bird is kind of nice. But forget birds for a minute! What did Ben say?*

It was beautiful, Emma sighed. *I was so proud of him. He looked so grown up, and he didn't cry at all until the end. And he sang. Do you believe that? For the first time ever in front of people. He stood up right in front of everyone, and he sang.*

Emma closed her eyes, and a little smile tugged at the corner of her lips. *He sang,* she sighed. *And he sounded wonderful. He hit every note. It was more perfect than any song I've ever heard, ever. My brother actually sang for me ... in front of everyone.*

Emma put her hand on the spot where her tattoo was and sighed, her eyes still shut tight. Aunt Pat sat in silence, too, until she noticed a tear begin to roll slowly down Emma's cheek. She slid over and folded Emma in her arms and lay next to her on the couch, gently stroking her hair. After a few minutes Duck jumped up and lay at her feet, and the three of them stayed that way for some time.

Tell me more, Aunt Pat finally said, gently. *It must have been a wonderful outpouring of love. And it was all for you, my angel. Who else talked?*

Paige went next, Emma said and, though she kept her eyes shut, she smiled a little, and her face started to light up again. *She said I loved my boobs! Do you believe that?* And now Emma giggled. *Trust Paige to talk about my boobs in church! She also talked about our favorite restaurant – hey, will I be able to go there ever again?*

You keep asking me stuff that you're going to have to figure out for yourself, Aunt Pat replied. *If it's important to you, I bet you'll find a way! But go on. Who else talked?*

Then Doug gave a speech, and it was really, really nice. He had a picture of me with Sarah's dog, Charlie, and he kept touching it and smiling. He cried, too, and it was hard to keep sitting in my tree. (Don't go there! warned Aunt Pat, with a laugh!) *I really wanted to let Doug know I was going to be just fine. I was really proud about everything he said 'cause he seemed really proud of me, and that felt so good. He talked about everyone at Town House, and they were all right there in the church. Turns out Doug closed Town House for the day, so how about that! Doug wants to be sure that the restaurant makes money and he NEVER closes, but they closed for me. For me!*

They must really love you, Aunt Pat said.

Oh, they do, said Emma matter of factly. *No one at Town House has to worry that I didn't know how much they care about me. We all know how special it is to work there – we're family! The Town House family! And Doug was great! He made people laugh, too, and that made me happy. I get that everyone has to be sad for a while. But I LOVE that they can laugh. Even my mom laughed at one point, but not during the speeches. It was before.*

Aunt Pat knew that the subject of Donna was a tricky one. Emma was just getting used to the fact that she was no longer on earth and, for the next several weeks, she needed to focus on getting settled into her new life. Thoughts of her family were going to be hard, but thoughts of her mom would be especially challenging.

Any mother-daughter relationship is special, but she knew that the Mommy-Emma relationship was especially poignant. Emma would be experiencing such complex feelings – worrying about the pain she caused her mom (despite the fact that dying was decidedly NOT her idea) and longing for her comforting touch, while at the same time working hard to pull away enough to live her life on her own.

It didn't help that these feelings, though intensified now, paralleled the struggle that Donna and Emma were beginning to face on earth as both prepared for the in-evitable time that Emma's impending adulthood would cause the empty nest that Donna dreaded almost from the first day she held her last baby in her arms.

Aunt Pat jumped on the idea that Donna had laughed, before Emma's thoughts wandered into a darker place. *What happened? What did your Mom find funny?*

Well, apparently Sarah worked for hours on a slide show that Mom wanted to play at the end of the funeral. They picked four of my favorite songs, and Sarah selected and re-selected every picture that showed the best times of my whole life from when I was a baby through to the time I was in Ireland. Ben put it together on his computer. Only it didn't work when they tried to load it on the funeral's computer. Ben was furious because he thought the church people were idiots – they apparently had their whole AV team working on it, and Ben kept saying that their AV team was a joke. They couldn't start the funeral because Mom wouldn't let them until they got the slides to work. Uncle Rusty was trying to help, and everyone was getting pretty testy. Finally, my mom sent Uncle Robert in to check on them because he's the only one that Rusty wouldn't yell at. He came back about a minute later and said that, just as he had gone into the room, one of the pastors said, "Don't worry everyone, I've got this under control," and Robert thought that he had figured out how to get the slides working. But, instead, he told everyone to bow their heads. "Dear Lord," he intoned solemnly, "if we ever needed your help, we need it now."

Robert quietly backed out before they saw him and, when he told Mom the story, she definitely laughed, albeit without much enthusiasm. "Oh, for heaven's sake," she sighed. "Ben, get in there and figure this out." Soon after that, they got it going ... kind of. When they played it at the end of my funeral, it cut off my face in a few of the pictures and focused mostly on my boobs but, since Paige pointed out how great they are, that seemed fine with everyone, and everyone was smiling and crying at the same time.

She and Patsy had a good chuckle over that, and Emma went on to tell her about the hauntingly beautiful song that Mel and Tommy sang. It was Leonard Cohen's version of *Hallelujah*, and she remembered as she watched that this was the version playing when Marissa Cooper died in the car crash on the *OC*. It was such a dramatic moment on the show, and she couldn't help but think that her death was probably every bit as dramatic in its own way, though she didn't have a boyfriend carry her from a burning car!

She was in awe of Mel's voice – she never heard her sing with more feeling – and Tommy looked so handsome standing up there playing his guitar like a pro. The whole audience was mesmerized, and Emma felt again a strange tingle of pride that she was the reason for all of her friends and family coming together, experiencing these moments that they would remember all of their lives.

She snuggled in closer to Aunt Pat. *You know,* she said, *I felt so strong looking in on all of those people. I felt ...* she giggled. *Well, I almost said that I felt like I could fly, but I probably could have seeing that I was a bird and all ... But you know what I mean. As people talked and hugged each other and cried and smiled, I felt like there was nothing I couldn't do.*

Love will do that, Patsy said. *I know lots of people have said this, but I often wonder why people wait until it's too late to tell people how much they meant to them.*

But that's not true, said Emma. *I knew. I think it was because it was so ... concentrated ... is that the right word? In my dad's part, he said something about me that I was thinking about all of them. He said, "EMMA plus ME equals BETTER ME" – wasn't that so sweet? But I was thinking almost exactly the same thing – the people in that room plus me made ME a BETTER ME ... wait is that too many "me's"? But you know what I mean. It was kind of awesome.*

Emma looked so peaceful and happy that Pat began to wonder if they should quit talking about the funeral while Emma was in such a good mood. As Emma continued to share what her dad said about her, Pat watched her closely for signs of heartache.

She wished that she had the wisdom that people associated with life after death because then she would know how best to shepherd Emma through the next several days ... but she didn't. She could only watch her carefully (but surreptitiously) and be there when Emma needed a hug or a home-cooked meal or just the presence of someone who adored her with a love that was growing every minute in both intensity and purity.

Pat realized that she was focused absolutely on Emma and her well-being and, in the short time they had been together, she had come to appreciate that her own death now had purpose. And the purpose was this ... to help this lovely child, who seemed so vulnerable in her confusion, to do her very best to surround her with the love she had experienced on earth, to keep her safe and light her way.

As Emma talked on, Pat pulled her tight to her chest and hoped her own beating heart would provide the wisdom and comfort that mere words could not.

Donna

Chapter 13

I am on auto-pilot. People speak to me, and I seem to be responding appropriately because no one looks at me funny or at least I don't notice if they do.

We have made it through the funeral, and Emma is gone. I found it remarkably easy to leave the church. I thought I would be the type that would throw myself over the casket and refuse to let them take it away. But I find that I am not thinking of Emma's body as Emma.

It's not that I am comforted that her spirit is in a better place. I simply do not believe that she could possibly be gone at all. Surely she will walk around the corner, strike a dramatic pose with her hand on her hips and say, *OMG, did you really think for one minute that I would leave you like that?* I think that's why I can't go near her room – can't even look down the hall at it. If I go in there and she's not in her bed, I will have to wonder where she is and whether she is safe.

I am proud that, at the wake, I seemed to find some pretense of "normal" – what in the world does that word even mean when your child is gone? I'm a talker, so words, even ones that are inane and meaningless, are important to me. After a few false starts that left me gasping for breath and surely embarrassed the people waiting to say how sorry they were, I happened upon words that seemed to work. They didn't prevent tears, but they didn't expose anyone to the despair that was bubbling just below the surface. *I don't regret a thing about the 19 years we had her,* I repeated over and over and over again. *She lived a full and wonderful life and packed a lot into such a short time.* I'd pause. *What I regret is all that she will miss in the future she will never have.* Elegant, heartfelt, appropriate.

But when I'm alone and the darkness returns, I find that these words might have been a lie. All I can think about is regret. Not for big things (though, if I conjure up the energy to think very hard, I might find a few). But there are plenty of little things that all feel overwhelmingly big right now.

The last time I saw Emma, I was walking to my office in London and Sarah was accompanying her to the airport for her flight home, alone. I was worried about her, but not abnormally so. She was the baby of the family, and I always worried about her. It's why I was so pleased when Sarah said she'd ride with her on the tube. She'd be safe with Sarah and, once she got on the plane, I was sure she'd sleep, and then Rod would be there and she'd slip back into summer Emma and all would be fine. I wouldn't have to worry again until she went back to school in the fall.

We parted at the station. I cried earlier that morning while I cooked her favorite breakfast (sadly, with English bacon instead of American, because I hadn't yet discovered that you could find American bacon if you looked hard enough). But I didn't cry when I actually said goodbye. I hugged her quickly and said something stupid like, *just go,* and I didn't make a big deal about her going. I had an "important" meeting that morning, or I would have taken her myself. And I was worried about my mascara running and looking bad for my "important" meeting, and I deliberately and methodically did not cry. We simply parted. I did sneak a peek at her as she walked away, and she was wiping her eyes (*I'm so sad because I don't know when I'll see Mom again*, she said later to Sarah), and I knew that she had let her tears come. But I didn't.

And I regret that moment. I regret not telling her how much I loved her and how much fun I had with her and how she always made everything so special and how proud I was of her and what was that eyebrow pencil she thought I would like? There would be plenty of time for all of that ...

Mom, I knew. I knew everything "just go" really meant. I knew that you were so happy for me, and I knew that you knew how happy I was. You were the one who made it so. I snuck a look back at you, too, and I saw you watching me, and I knew all that you wanted to say.

The last time I spoke to Emma was Wednesday – a week after that morning – and she was rushed. She was cleaning her room and trying to get ready to go out, and I was a little annoyed because she was distracted. And what was the point of facetiming if I couldn't see her lovely face? I used the line that Sarah had taught us was code for "I don't really want to talk anymore" – *Let me let you go* – and she didn't laugh, but just said, *Okay*. And I let my irritation bubble up and, though I said *I love you*, I remember clearly that I didn't say it with much feeling. I almost called her back, but I knew we would talk again soon. There would be plenty of time to say it with meaning ...

I heard it the way you would have wanted me to. I knew how lucky I was that we both said it every single time we talked. The words weren't the thing, Mom. The feelings were the thing, and I knew. I always knew. Even when you were mad at me, I knew.

The last night that Emma lived was the next night, and she and Ben and Sarah skyped for a long time and, as I lay in bed tossing and turning, thinking of the full day I had the next day, I chose not to get up and join them. It was midnight in London, and it seemed like too much an effort. I did hear them laughing, and I did think how lucky I was that my children always had so much to say to each other. But I didn't get up. There would be plenty of time to join in the laughter in the days and weeks and years ahead ...

Partly we laughed about you and how funny you are and how much we love you. You were there with us, Mom. You are always wherever one of us is. You're here with me now.

But wait. Regret? Emma can't really be gone ... not today ... not forever ... things like this don't happen to my family ... not to this child ... it couldn't possibly be real ... we can't be a family without her ... everyone has a place, everyone has a role ... without the vibrant "we" that was, we will never be again ... and that's just not possible ... not in this family ...

When I'm not numb, I think I might be angry. But with whom am I angry? Emma? Perhaps I'm angry with Emma. *How could you just leave us? Where have you gone? How could you possibly die with no warning? How could you die when I wasn't even there?* Had I been there, surely you would have stayed. Would I have realized that you weren't yourself, and would I have taken you to the doctor and insisted that they work harder to discover why you were so tired? Oh, God, am I angry with myself? Or with Rod – *are you sure she was okay that night?* Or with Paige – *you saw her that night. How could she just lie down and die?*

Mom, don't be angry with me. I couldn't help it. I just went to sleep. I couldn't have known. I wouldn't have ever chosen to leave you. No one's to blame. It must have just been my time. Don't shut me out. I love you so much.

I said, *No, no autopsy,* and I said it was because I couldn't bear to have them cut you up, and surely that was part of it. But was part of it also that, if somehow your most-awesome-trip-ever had anything at all to do with your dying, I would have to just curl up and die, too? Could I take a chance that thoughts of that magical week would somehow give way to a BIG regret that the long plane ride had loosened something in you that found its way to your heart and took you away from us? Should I have said, *No,* to the assignment and stayed home to cook you bacon?

Oh, Emma, where are you?

It's late afternoon. Rod is rousing me because I must have told someone that I would go to the balloon release that her friends had planned. Perhaps Emma will be there ... this is the kind of thing for which she would have been totally front and center. Can I take seeing her friends, so vibrant, so alive, amidst the color and lightness and happy symbolism of balloons? Will I wish one of them, any of them, was gone instead of Emma? If I start down that path, will I ever be able to pull myself back?

We arrive at Paige's house and Paige's mom, Susan, is pouring soda for the "champagne" toast, and Emma's closest friends are all blowing up balloons and drawing pictures and writing private messages on them. Some need two balloons because they have so much to say. Rusty draws pictures of her two tattoos, which was a big deal for him because he hated them so. It is the closest he can come to saying what a great kid Emma was despite the tattoos, and perhaps he is sorry that he gave her such a hard time. Some friends are laughing and some friends are crying quietly and some friends are hugging.

I feel like I am seeing this from a great distance. Your absence is everywhere. When was the last time Paige had people over and you weren't there? I am trying to be the Mrs. Mebane that these kids know and love, but I can't seem to find her, so I nod and try to smile and try to hug back.

They give me a special balloon that you will somehow know is mine – it has a smiley face on it and is all silver and glittery. I write, "I will hold you in my heart until I can hold you in my arms again." Not very profound. Could I have said more if I could somehow pull myself out of the mist? No, I don't think I will ever have anything to say again.

As the sun sets, we go outside to the edge of the golf course that borders Paige's back yard. Susan starts a count down, pauses because she is crying too hard, then restarts. On the group shoutout – *To Emma!* – we release the balloons in unison. The brightly colored messages rise, hesitantly at first, but then they quickly gather in an air stream as a pack. They bob with purpose in a northwesterly direction (Rod later announced that he now knows precisely where heaven is) into the sunset.

I feel strange. Though I am still feeling a sense of distance – almost like being outside of myself, observing with dispassion the part of me that is still functioning – I do feel a connection with this feeling of hope that emanates from the group around me. It is a peaceful moment, a beautiful moment even. I sense that it will only last until I can see the last of the balloons, and I strain my eyes to see for as long as I can. Emma, are you there?

I'm here Mom. The balloons surround me. I am reading all of the messages, and I am happy. I see yours, and I grasp it. I will keep it close to me. Your peace makes me stronger. Hold on to it as long as you can. It helps me, Mom, to believe that you will be okay. I need for you to be okay. I need for you to be Mom.

The balloons are gone, and I am numb again. Emma's friends are going to order pizza and (we learn later) do a DVD of all their favorite memories of Emma. I am not ready for Emma to be a memory. I need to go home and avoid her room and her cat and her car parked in the driveway and all of the pockets of her that now signify nothing. I am devoid of color, of hope, of life.

Emma, where are you? Where have you gone?

Emma

Chapter 14

I'm not feeling well, Emma said quietly. *I'm so tired.*

You do look a little pale, replied Patsy.

I felt so strong when I was reading all the balloons. I felt like I could do anything.

Then why do you think you're so tired now?

I don't know, but I think it might have something to do with my mom. She is just so sad, and I can't seem to connect with her like I did with my dad in the hospital. For a minute, I felt her love and then it disappeared, and all I could feel was bad stuff – she seems almost angry, and I don't get it. I get that she's sad, but when I try to connect with her it just feels dark.

As Emma said those last words, she seemed to disappear a little around the edges, and Aunt Pat grew genuinely concerned. She suggested that Emma lie down on the couch and try to rest. Emma closed her eyes and disappeared a little more. Just as Aunt Pat began to panic a little, she heard a deep voice.

Hi Pat. We met once at Rod and Donna's wedding. I'm Tom Mebane, and I think you may need me to take a look at Emma.

Pat knew that Dr. Mebane had been a pediatrician nearly all his life, and she almost collapsed with relief that he had come. His very presence seemed to perk Emma up a little.

Grandpa, she exclaimed. *How did you get here?*

When someone exhibits a need that intensifies beyond the typical every day ebbs-and-flows of his or her current condition, the molecular structure of a reactor to that need can shift just enough that it – or in this case I – can re-form into a presence that can be experienced as a reality.

Patsy and Emma looked at each other, and Emma smiled and gave a little shrug. She loved Grandpa Mebane, but she rarely understood what he said. If he wasn't talking in big words, he was asking her crazy stuff like how she thought the president was doing or what kids her age were doing to try to save the planet. It wasn't that he was a snob or anything. Just really smart and really curious about EVERYTHING!

She remembered one time, a few years before he died, he had asked her in all seriousness what it was like to smoke pot. Now how do you respond to a question like that from your grandfather? *Uh, I'm not sure?* she tried and, thankfully, that had ended that. He was definitely weird. *(Come to think of it, was that where Dad got it?)* But she felt safe with him and was relieved that he had somehow arrived on the scene just when she seemed to need him the most.

Let's have a look, Grandpa said, and he dug around in his little black bag. He listened to her heart and took her temperature and even tapped on her knee a little bit. He shone a light in her eyes and looked in her ears and, just as she was beginning to think this was all for show, he declared that he knew what the problem was.

There are energy sources and energy drains and eventually you will learn to balance the two. Right now, however, you are still too new at this to harness the positive and neutralize the negative.

Although she didn't want to hurt his feelings, Emma knew that this was important stuff and that this was no time to pretend she understood something she didn't. *Grandpa,* she said. *I don't know what you're saying!*

I'm saying that you are going to have to be very selective about how you interact with the people you have left behind. I'm guessing that you have been spending time with your family and friends. You need to be very cautious about that. You can't just be gallivanting around down there. There are certain rules that must be followed. And for sure you need to avoid situations that have the potential to jeopardize your own happiness.

Emma thought for a minute. *Are you saying that I shouldn't spend time with my family?*

Grandpa responded gently, *No, no, my dear. You have already discovered that there are certain situations that can be very positive. Handled cautiously, connecting can be good for the people who love you and certainly can help you. But the risk is great, particularly so soon after your transition, that you will touch something you can't handle. The whole bird thing? That was perfect. You were able to feel the positive energy, and people who were ready got to see you in a form that, quite frankly, wouldn't be unsettling to them.*

How did I make that happen? asked Emma, who thought she might start warming up to the idea of being a bird if it meant she could look in on her family regularly.

There's no magic formula. Certain conditions exist that enable a connection. You cannot manufacture these or will them into being because you want something badly enough. Over time, you will come to understand the connection to the tools you have, and you will be able to harness your power and use it as an instrument to achieve your desires. At the same time that you are learning your powers, you must work to start to diminish the needs that are associated with your earthly life.

Grandpa paused because he noticed that Emma was glazing over a bit. *I guess I'm saying that you need to find a balance between keeping connections to your earthly life and living a new life here. Over time, more and more of your focus should be on your new world.*

But I don't know anybody here, sighed Emma. *No disrespect to you, Patsy, but I don't think we can be together 24/7. I need friends, I need to have fun, I need to have a life.*

Exactly, Grandpa smiled, *Now you're cooking with gas! Focus on all that can be, not on all that was. What was is gone, sweetie, and though you can touch it, you can't have it. It will feel a little sad sometimes at first, but you will only be sad until you start to experience all of the wonderful aspects of your new life.*

Emma looked unconvinced. *Are there only dead people here?* And, even though she didn't want to imply she didn't like dead people, it was hard to muster up a lot of enthusiasm.

Yes, Grandpa answered, *but dead people are people, too. And every bit as real as they were on earth. It's just that the reality is different, that's all. Some of the differences will immediately feel right to you, and you'll wonder why that's not how things have always been. Some will be a little harder to get used to. Is there anything that has seemed better to you so far?*

Emma giggled, *Well, shopping without money is pretty cool! And I am so, so happy to have Duck again.*

At that, Duck thumped his tail and wiggled over for an ear scratch. He sighed with pleasure as Emma loved with him, and she felt the same sense of peace and even awe that she had when she had first reconnected with him.

You see, said Grandpa. *You haven't been here that long, and you've already discovered some of the joys of this world. What about communication tools? Have you figured out how to "speak" with your friends back home?*

Emma definitely brightened. *Well, I can still read Facebook and right now it's all about me still, so that's definitely kind of awesome. And, when I was a bird, I could clearly hear everything that everyone was saying. Is that what you mean?*

Yes, but when you get a little stronger, you will also be able to communicate back. This is definitely trickier, but you will learn to do it. I know you will. I have confidence in you. I always thought you were the Mebane with the most gumption. I know you worried that you weren't that smart. But you are, my dear. I think you're going to do just fine. I believe in you.

Emma beamed. *Oh, Grandpa, thank you. You've made me feel so much better.*

There was a lull in the conversation as Grandpa started to pack up his bag. *Will you be staying here?* Emma finally asked sweetly, although she kind of hoped he would say no. Patsy was one thing, but a daily Grandpa presence might be a little too much.

No, sweetie. I have places to go and people to see. I'm back to full time doctoring while I wait for Grandma to join me.

As Emma hugged Grandpa and kissed him goodbye, she said, *I feel like I'm going to have a lot of questions, but I can't really think of any more right now. Will you be back?*

You can connect with me anytime you need me, sweetie.

But how do I do that? asked Emma.

How do you think you might do it? asked Grandpa right back, and Emma groaned inwardly. Her brain was definitely starting to hurt from all the thinking she had been doing. Nevertheless, she considered a few options because she didn't want Grandpa to go away before she had figured out how to get him back!

After a few minutes, she grinned. *My car!* She exclaimed. (Grandpa had given it to her for her 16th birthday, which happened to coincide with him thinking he had gotten too old to drive.)

There's my girl, Grandpa said with a twinkle in his eye. *You see ... you are going to be just fine!* And with a kiss and a pat on her head, he disappeared.

Jason

Chapter 15

It was late morning, after everyone had picked at some food for breakfast, when Sarah declared, *I'm ready to get my tattoo now.* She immediately got the attention of the assembled group and continued, *I've been thinking "what would Emma want" and that's what she would want ...*

Stunned silence followed. Finally Donna spoke. *Honey, I'm not sure that's the best idea right now. It's only been a week, and you may not be thinking clearly.*

No, insisted Sarah. *I'm doing it. I know it's what Emma wanted. Don't you remember how she bugged me about it all the time? She'd say, "Sarah, pllleeeaasse get a tattoo with me. It would be so cool to have the same one as you." And I'd say, "Emma, there are tattoo people, and that would be you, and there are non-tattoo people, and that would be me." When we were in London, she and I were shopping while you were at work, and we passed a tattoo parlor. She begged me to "just go look." She said we didn't have to get one that day, but insisted that all she wanted for her 21st birthday was for us to get ones that matched.*

Jason, who had been pacing around in the kitchen wondering when he should crack open the first beer of the day pitched in. *Let's do it!*

Mom, still a little skeptical, asked, *But what kind of tattoo would you get?*

Well, that's just it, Sarah said, her voice choking. *While we were looking at the choices, I said, "But the thing is, Emma,*

And so there was a layer of hope wedged between the grief and the regret, and he was almost horrified that any positive feeling would spring from the death of his baby sister. He tried not to make this about him, but there were times when there were so many emotions bubbling up and around that he drifted into not thinking of Emma at all. Then he would jolt himself back into the absence of her, and his feelings would all blend into a grief so powerful that the only way to keep from going insane was to talk and to pace and to drink more beer.

So, *hell, yeah,* he was up for getting a tattoo, and it had nothing to do with the tattoo. It had everything to do with a physical symbol that they all belonged together and, for better or for worse, they were each part of the same family unit.

At 4:00, Donna, Sarah, Jason, Whitney, Ben, and Alex all bundled into the car. Poor Rod had recently promised Emma that he would take Juice to the vet because his teeth seemed to be bothering him, and he had already made an appointment at 4:30. Since tattoos were not part of his bond with Emma and taking care of Juice was, he felt that he would be letting her down to reschedule. Besides, he had not taken part in the intensive planning and, though he was not philosophically opposed to tattoos, he wanted to spend some time thinking through the best symbol of a permanent connection to his little girl.

The tattoo parlor could have been a movie set it was so perfectly stereotypic and SO not Mebane. Loud heavy metal music was playing, and there was a vile movie that clearly was rated X for sex on the TV in the waiting room. Two huge snakes slithered in an aquarium along the wall, and the Sons of Anarchy or their close relatives kept popping in and out to hug a scary looking fellow named, Casey, who had tattoos and piercings over his entire body and seemed to be the person in charge. He was also apparently the one with whom they had their appointments, although you would never know it from the attention he paid them – glancing their way occasionally with a look that could only be interpreted as dismissive.

After an hour or so, Mom grew tired of trying to avert her eyes from the TV sex and approached Casey. *Excuse me,* she said in her I'm-saying-this-sweetly-but-don't-test-me voice. *We had an appointment an hour ago.*

Casey seemed amused. *You don't say. Well, sadly, we're a little behind as you can clearly see. I have one more person before you.*

There's six of us, Mom said, *and we'll need to go ahead and get started soon.*

Of course, Casey replied. He smiled, which gave him a bit of a sinister look and repeated, slowly, *I have one more before you.*

Mom flomped back down in the folding chair and seemed to cave inwards a little after exerting the energy required to get nowhere with Casey. Jason could tell that she was barely holding it together. The luster was definitely wearing off what seemed like such a good idea that morning, and the horror of the last week was always a threat to overtake the outward appearance of "normal" that they were trying so hard to maintain.

Jason sensed that he was the one who could be a hero in this kind of setting, and he took Casey aside. *Listen man. I don't know if anyone mentioned this, but we're doing this because my little sister died last week. We just had her funeral yesterday, and we're all still a little raw.*

Casey visibly softened up. *No problem, man. Let me see if Tommy can take over here, and I'll get to you guys real soon. Just let me go have a smoke, man, and we'll get started ...*

And get started they did. Sarah boldly decided to go first. Truth be known, though the others had come up with what they wanted, it wasn't at all clear that any of them would really go through with it. Sarah had the best shot since this was her idea and she was the only one Emma had really worked on to get "inked" (as they now knew was the cool way to say it).

She filled out the paperwork (more extensive, it seemed, than for major surgery) and described what she wanted ... a star like Emma's with a stream of smaller stars behind it. Casey drew a sketch, and they discussed it. *Can you make it smaller?* Sarah asked, and Casey drew another sketch. *Can you make it even smaller?* Sarah asked. *I'm a professional, and I really can't have a tattoo showing while I do my job.*

Casey tried a few more, each time with the same result. *Look,* he said finally, and the smile was a little sinister looking again. *Do you even want a tattoo?*

Not really, said Sarah. *I'm a professional.*

I'm a professional, too, said Casey with a bit of an edge. *Trust me. This is going to be just fine.* And it was!

Turns out tattoos take far longer than you'd expect and hurt just about as much as you'd expect. But, through her tears, Sarah kept smiling and nodding at her family members who were huddled together in the small room holding her hand or touching her shoulder or looking her in the eyes and saying how brave she was.

And, when she was finished, she looked almost radiant, and Jason had a flashback to all of the times she had made him proud when they were growing up.

I'll go now, said Mom. She had brought in Emma's Town House time card that Emma herself had filled out and signed *(could it have only been just eight days ago?)*, and Mom decided that she wanted to have a little piece of Emma on her wrist forever. Casey was almost gentle with her as they created a design that, in addition to Emma's signature, included a star (they had all decided that a star would be what connected them) and a balloon that Casey said he hoped would bring her some peace.

She said she wouldn't cry – she had cried so much, and getting a tattoo was after all only physical pain. At one point, as Casey told her she was doing great and she responded that it was good to have pain somewhere other than her heart, Jason noticed that Casey paused to wipe his own tears away, and the family circle opened up temporarily to pull him in.

Someone suggested that they do some shots, and Casey found a bottle of his best bourbon, and they all raised their glasses to Emma.

Ben went next. His tattoo ideas had become increasingly elaborate over the hours leading up to the appointment. He went from saying he'd go for moral support ... to agreeing to go to get a really small one ... to sketching out a montage that took up most of his upper left arm.

In truth, the design was stunning: a beautiful piece of art. The central theme was music – the shared love of which had sealed his bond with Emma. At its center was an airplane with a gramophone body and keyboard wings – the symbol of his all-time favorite band and their signature album, Neutral Milk Hotel's *In the Aeroplane Over the Sea*. Of course, in keeping with the family theme, there was a star shining high above the plane and, below that, there were ashes falling from the sky. The ashes formed the dates of Emma's life, written in her own hand, traced carefully by Casey onto Ben's arm. Last to be etched was the title of another of Ben and Emma's favorite albums, this one by Bon Iver – *For Emma Forever Ago*.

Even before Emma's death, these albums had been an important source of comfort for Ben. He had regularly connected with the sorrowful yet strangely uplifting emotions the lyrics elicited, and it seemed that the songs anchored both his best and worst times for as long as he could remember. One stanza seemed especially poignant now that Emma was gone, and it came from *In the Aeroplane Over the Sea*'s title song.

> *One day we will die*
> *And our ashes will fly*
> *From the aeroplane over the sea.*
> *But for now we are young,*
> *Let us lay in the sun*
> *And count every beautiful thing we can see.*

Mom laid down right next to Ben so she could comfort him from the pain that she knew firsthand would only partly be from the sting of the needle. Alex – who had known and loved Emma before becoming friends with Ben and thus was a living link between them – stood on his other side, and Jason, Whitney, and Sarah sat on the floor.

At one point, after nearly an hour had passed and just when they all had begun to worry that Ben would not be able to endure another minute, the rock music that had been playing incessantly in the background suddenly stopped. And in the blessed silence that followed, Jason reached out and touched Ben's outstretched hand. *You can do this, boy* (a name of endearment Jason hadn't used in years), and Ben looked right into his eyes and smiled. A sense of harmony enveloped them, and even Casey paused to enjoy the moment (and to sneak in another shot of bourbon).

After a while, Casey started again, and so did the music. But instead of Led Zeppelin or Guns N' Roses or Nirvana, a lovely song they had never heard started to play softly. Because it was so different than the god-awful noise that had preceded it for hours, they all noticed it and, when Mom heard the words "shine on," she asked Casey what the song was.

He said he had never heard it before, so she asked Jason to go investigate. They all joked that it must be Emma but stopped when Mom started to cry. She quickly turned back to Ben and told Casey to go on because it just had to be a coincidence, and she didn't want to sink back into the haze that she had only just pulled herself out of to make Sarah happy.

Jason meanwhile tried everything to figure out what the song was. Shazam didn't recognize it, and none of the bikers present had ever heard it, and no one seemed to even know quite where the sound system was or whether there was a radio on somewhere.

Jason tried to memorize a few of the lines, but being unused to bourbon didn't help his memory. And, just as he found a pen, the song stopped. He had a sinking feeling he failed the task his mom assigned but vowed that he would somehow find the song someday. He went back in the room to fess up, but Mom had clearly moved on, and soon it was his turn and he forgot about the phantom song and gave into his nerves a bit.

He really had very little intention of getting a tattoo, but at this point he and Casey were practically best friends, and he wasn't going to be the one to wuss out. He and Casey worked for a long time on his design and, when it was complete, he really was quite proud of it and the way it brought together the Grateful Dead, whom he truly loved, and Emma, whom he wished he had allowed himself to love more. After another toast to Emma, he lay down and, though Mom didn't lie next to him, the family gathered around in the same way they had with the others, and he felt truly happy for the first time in a long time.

The evening wore on. They had a hasty dinner of pizza which Mom arranged to have delivered, and they shared it with the even-more-extended family that now included the bikers. At one point, there was a half-hour pause when Whitney passed out. (She, too, was unused to bourbon, but they also discovered on the internet afterwards that the top of a foot is the most painful place to get a tattoo, so she hadn't needed to apologize as much as she did.)

At close to 1:00 in the morning, Casey finally finished with Alex whose 19 stars up and down her forearm they all had agreed were particularly beautiful. By this time, Casey considered it an honor to have inked them and refused payment, but they insisted and as he printed the care directions that Mom had obsessed about, he urged them to come back to visit any time.

And for most of that long, long evening, the Mebane family proved that they could still be the Mebane family even with Jason and even without Emma and, for that little respite, they were all profoundly grateful. After hugs and kisses all around, they piled back into the car to face the trip back into darkness.

Emma

Chapter 16

Emma tried to follow Grandpa's advice. She really did! After he left, she decided then and there that she was going to go out and explore her new world, but she just wanted to read a few Facebook posts first for a little courage.

She was shocked and amazed when Sarah posted a picture of the tattoo she had just gotten. *OMG, this is the best thing EVER,* she declared as she ran out to the car and headed to the tattoo parlor. She may have been happier in her whole life but, at the moment, she couldn't think of when. *She did it,* Emma laughed, *she really did it! That is totally my sister.*

She followed a biker into the shop and crowded into the little room with her family just as Ben took off his shirt and lay down on the table. *Unbelievable!* Her brother was getting a tattoo. And, though she avoided looking too closely at her mom given both her last experience and Grandpa's advice, she did notice that her wrist was bandaged and knew that she had gotten one as well. *Too totally cool.*

Guys, you are the best family EVER, she said, trying to get someone to hear her. *I'm so happy. Thank you so, so much,* she repeated several times to each person in the room but, no matter what she tried, she couldn't get anyone's attention.

Despite her earlier distaste, she closed her eyes and willed herself to be a bird, but when she opened her eyes, she was still just plain Emma.

She hopped up onto the paint chest in the corner and watched for a while, hoping an idea would come to her. After a few minutes, she gave up and let herself become absorbed into the happiness that surrounded her. She felt the surging strength that she now knew was a result of something good happening for her family and, as she watched Casey's kindnesses multiply and the laughs flow freely, she sighed with a feeling of absolute completeness.

She was a part of this family, and she understood with unshakable clarity that she always would be no matter the distance and the worlds between them. Her family had made her who she was, but she had shaped them, too. And that, she suddenly knew in the very core of her being, was a bond that would last for all eternity!

After what seemed hours, though, she got a little restless just sitting in the corner. She was also feeling hot from the small room and was starting to get a bit of a headache from the loud rock music that was playing continuously. She decided to go explore.

She started opening closets, but didn't find much of interest until she saw an iPod sitting in a docking station tucked away on the counter in the kitchen. It seemed to be the source of the awful music that was giving her such a headache. *I wonder if I could figure out how to turn it off,* she thought. As she started trying to make her hand have some kind of impact on the iPod, she suddenly had an inspiration.

Wouldn't it be hilarious, she thought, *if I could find a way to have my family hear the song that played when I got MY first tattoo.* After all, this would be their first (and likely only) tattoo.

Emma was sure that at least Sarah and her mom would recognize the song if she could figure out a way to make it play. And, as she thought about it, she realized that this might be just the idea she was searching for. Could she somehow "send" a song to her family to let them know that she was there with them and that what they were doing was absolute perfection? Could she somehow "cross over" and make Casey's iPod play what she wanted it to?

After working for several minutes, she managed to coordinate her hand movements well enough to pull the iPod out of the docking station, and all of a sudden the shop was (blessedly) filled with the sound of silence. However, try as she might, she could not get her fingers to work well enough on the device to pull up a song list and to find just the right one to send.

She was about to give up in frustration when she remembered the phone message she got on the first morning she woke up in this new world. The annoying voice asked whether she had forgotten the rules and suggested that she try music. *Hmmm.*

So, she pulled out her own iPhone and searched for the perfect song. She still thought the "first tattoo" song would be hilarious, but she decided that she wanted to send something more meaningful that would also let her family know that she understood the importance of the moment. She thought hard and, after a few minutes, had a flash of brilliance.

Stars, she thought. *They're all getting something with stars.* How perfect that a star would be a permanent symbol of their everlasting connection. (And how brilliant of her to think of it!) *It has to have "shine" in it*, she thought and selected the first song she found that fit the bill. It was an obscure little song from a group that she had discovered just recently and hadn't had a chance even to tell Ben about yet.

She hit PLAY and held her breath ...

And it played. It didn't just play, it rang out through the whole shop. She ran back to the room to see if anyone was getting it, and she was thrilled to see that everyone had stopped what they were doing and were listening to the song ... to her song ... to the very first message she was able to send.

She was thrilled. *Okay,* she thought, *I can live with this. It's not perfect, but I can make it better with practice.*

But, even as she watched, she saw her Mom dismiss the idea that the song was anything more than a coincidence and, though Mom dispatched Jason to investigate, she told Casey to keep going with Ben.

Oh, Mom, she sighed in exasperation. *You're killing me!* Still, she decided to declare success and keep feeling good about this. It was her first time, and she could tell that she had made an important connection with Ben, Sarah, and Jason, and even with Alex and Whitney.

This is good, she decided. *This is really good. I can do this, I know I can,* and she plopped back down on the paint

cabinet, congratulating herself that this had been a pretty
darn good first week!

Sarah

Chapter 17

Sarah knew that she had to drive back to Washington soon. It seemed a century ago that she had left her car in Geneva, before she flew to London with Emma. She could hardly imagine how she was going to be able to pull herself together for the long drive home.

But she knew, if she didn't leave soon, that she never would and, though there were parts of that that felt right, she had lived her whole life being responsible, and walking away from her job ... from her whole career ... was not responsible, even if your sister had just died.

Her mom didn't want to go into Emma's room, but Sarah didn't want to leave it. She was comforted by having Emma all around her. She lay on Emma's bed, touched her things, sat at her makeup table. She sprayed on her perfume and stared at the pictures on her walls. Like her mom, she checked Facebook every few minutes and cried at every new entry, even those that were supposed to be hopeful.

How odd to feel such pure sadness, she thought. There is no one to be angry with, no drunk driver to hate. There is no tiny piece of the relief that comes from losing someone who had suffered through some kind of illness.

In her email to work, she said she felt some small comfort in how Emma died. In fact, she said, if someone had come to her and told her that her sister had to die and there was nothing she could do to change it, but that she could pick how she would go, she would have picked "relax to death" in her sleep, in her own bed, surrounded by the things she loved.

Sarah would have tried to bargain, of course. She'd only have picked that Emma die as she did if Sarah couldn't die instead ... or trade every possession she had ever owned ... or exchange Emma's life for 10,000 people she didn't know (which was a dilemma posed by the *Would you rather ...?* game that she and Emma sometimes played).

She was a psychologist, and she had been taught about how to handle situations like this. But she seemed to have forgotten everything she ever learned. She simply couldn't wrap her head around it. How could she start processing through Emma's death when she couldn't even accept it? Emma simply could not be gone forever. Emma was so much a part of her life ... she was such an important piece of the whole that was her family. Several of her friends had noted at one time or another that *to love one Mebane was to love them all.* Well, by extension, if you lost one Mebane, would they all be lost?

Everyone had a particular role in a family, everyone was "the" something. In her family, her mom was "the *nurturing* one," her dad "the *eccentric* one," Jason "the *rebellious* one," Ben "the *kind* one." She supposed that people thought of her as "the *smart* one."

And Emma? Even strangers knew that she was "the ... *fun* one." Her personality was so strong that most people labeled her whole family "fun," and Sarah worried that they now wouldn't be fun ever again, and what would her family become? What would the new label be? The "sad" family? The "unlucky" family? The family that had lost a child? Are you even still a family when you have lost such a huge part of yourselves?

Although she knew it was too early to hope for such a thing, she still felt disappointed that her family was not pulling together in the same way that they had for all of the other important milestones of their lives. Instead, they seem to have retreated into remote corners of their own souls, searching for a way to keep living.

Jason went home to Seattle. Ben went back to work, though God was that hard. As he said to Mom, *the people at your work thought they knew Emma. The people at mine really did.* But he was loyal to Doug, and Doug had lost Emma, too, and they all had to chip in to fill her shifts until they could rouse themselves to think of a permanent replacement.

Mom mostly lay in bed and stared at the walls. She cried all the time and only got up because she had to pee and every once in a while to eat. She considered it a good day if she brushed her teeth or took a bath. Dad was busy, busy all the time, trying to save pieces of Emma. He was organizing Emma's computer files and her photos and her HeyTells and her games and anything she had ever touched. It was almost as though he was afraid that, if he paused for a moment, something would slip through the cracks and be lost forever.

Sarah wished she could help. She was a helper by nature. But she couldn't. She didn't have the strength. Whatever energy she had she spent trying to be her own therapist. *Maybe,* she reasoned, *if I can help myself, I can eventually help my family.*

One thing she knew was important was to talk about your feelings. Despite the fog that surrounded them, they did still seem to be able to do that. She would often go lie down next to Mom, and they would talk. It was too soon to speak of Emma as a memory, but they found ways to talk about her as though she was almost still a present tense. Dad had given them the language of this when he challenged them all to think in terms of *what Emma would want*. And so there were a lot of statements like *Emma would be saying this or doing that.* Sometimes, they would simply say, *I just can't believe this,* and that was often enough to keep the deep well of grief at bay long enough to breathe for a while. So, one strategy for surviving – talk about your feelings – she could check off the list. They had that covered.

Sarah's friends also rallied in an amazing way. They came to grieve and stayed to help and were always, always instantly on the other end of a phone call or a Wall post. She knew she wouldn't be able to speak at Emma's funeral, but her friend Erin did on her behalf.

Erin recalled that, the first time she met Sarah, she mentioned having a sister named Emma, and how Erin understood from that moment how special their bond was. She spoke of how they were so different but complemented each other perfectly. She talked of Emma's beauty, her vast capacity for forgiveness and her compassion – *Emma was the kind of girl,* she noted, *who wouldn't recline her seat in an airplane for fear of taking someone else's leg space.* She spoke of her humor and her sparkle and how her "mishaps" were a source of the constant laughter between them.

Erin captured Sarah's love of Emma perfectly, and she and Maureen and Sarah R. and Allison and all of her work friends were there for her in whatever way she needed without her even asking. Yes, she could check off another strategy – connect with a support group and stay connected even when you are too tired to ask for help.

It was another strategy for living with grief that gave Sarah the push she needed finally to make the decision to leave home to go "home." She knew that she had to re-establish a routine, and that was not going to be possible in Geneva. And so, one day, she left. With just her dad available to give a Mebane Send-off, she got in the car with her dogs and drove away.

She cried the whole way. She had bought a tape recorder in the hopes that she could use it to keep talking, keep sharing her feelings even when there was no one listening. She tried to use it on the way home, but it was too soon to trade the comfort of her family for the impersonality of a machine. As she drove, however, a new idea began to form.

What if, she thought, *I pretend that I am talking to Emma?* I know she wouldn't answer me, but perhaps there would be some comfort in still talking to her. As the hours passed and she drew closer to what would be the next phase of her life – her life-without-Emma phase – she warmed up to the idea. *Yes*, she decided. *Someone has taken her away from me, but no one can take me away from her.*

I'll do it, she decided. I'll use my tape recorder to call her every night. I'll still tell her about my day and imagine what she'd say. I'll put her picture on my kitchen table and light a candle and pour a glass of wine, and I'll call her on my tape recorder!

Though she still wept, a tiny part of her began to feel empowered by this idea. There may never be new Emma stories but, like it or not, there could still be Sarah stories and for that she hoped she would someday be grateful.

Sisters

Chapter 18

SOUND OF TAPE RECORDER BEING TURNED ON

SILENCE ... MUFFLED SOBBING ... SILENCE ... SNIFFLING ...
NOSE BLOWING ... LOUD SOBBING ... SILENCE

SOUND OF TAPE RECORDER BEING TURNED OFF ... THEN
BACK ON

(SOFTLY) *Hi, Emma.*

SOBBING ... LONG SILENCE ... SNIFFLING ... SOBBING ...
SILENCE

SOUND OF TAPE RECORDER BEING TURNED OFF

>>>>

*Oh, man. Try again, Sarah! You can do this. I know you
can. I know you think I can't hear you, but I can. This is a
terrific idea. I am so psyched! I've already decided that I'm
going to do the same thing. I'm going to tell you all about my
day and pretend you can hear me, too. Same time every night.
I'm at the dining room table now and I have your picture set
up and a candle lit. And – awesome – I'm even having a glass
of wine!*

*I'll start since you're having trouble getting going.
Heeeeyyyyy. It's me, Emma. I feel like we haven't talked for a
while, so there's a lot to get you caught up on. First thing I
want to say is I am sooooo excited about your tattoo. Just so
you know, it was me that sent the song. I was there!! Isn't that
cool? I love yours. It's a little small, but that's okay. It's a star,
so I almost feel like we got it together!*

I'm doing okay here. Aunt Pat is with me, and she's really fun and cool, and we've been shopping and hanging out. Grandpa Mebane also came to see me, and he's just the same. He's so weird and fun, and he helped me understand some stuff.

But maybe even the best of all? Duck is here. Do you believe it? He was so happy to see me. We've been attached at the hip ever since I first woke up AFTER ... By the way, I've decided to call my first 19 years BEFORE and since that night AFTER. It seems more sensitive to everyone's feelings. That way I don't have to say anything about ... you know ... me dying and all.

I gotta go because I told Duck I would take him to the dog park, and he's dancing around like he does with about 10 dog toys in his mouth. But I'll be here tomorrow, same time, same place. I love you. You can do this.

〉〉〉〉

Okay, Emma. I'm going to try this again. So, this is way, way harder than I could possibly even imagine it would be. If I cared about anyone but you right now, it would make me feel bad that I wasn't nicer to people who had lost someone. I mean, I think I'm better than most. I'm in "the business" of helping people. But I can't help thinking that none of them was as special as you are or have the relationship we have. People tell me they think of their loss every day – every day, I think of nothing else. I am trying to pretend I care about what is happening around me and that I am "in the moment," but I'm not. I'm with you. I only care about you. I only want to be with you.

I broke up with Matt. I know, right? It seemed like we were on to something, and I know you're disappointed for me. But, really, I don't want to be with anyone except people who knew and loved you or maybe a few who just know me and love me, but they have to love me a lot. I can occasionally be with people who don't know me at all or know me only a little but don't know about you ... although, with them, I sometimes want to scream that they shouldn't be smiling or talking or walking or being "normal" because nothing will ever be normal again.

So, all in all, I'm kind of a mess. I know this hasn't been that great of a conversation, but it's the best I can do right now. I love you and will call you tomorrow. Maybe I can do better.

>>>>

Aw, Sarah. I wish with all my heart that I hadn't made everyone so sad. Maybe you should get a hot tub. I know that sounds crazy, but you can't imagine what's happened to ours! It's huge. Honestly, Aunt Pat and I can practically swim in it, and I go and be in it when I'm feeling really sad, and I close my eyes and you're almost with me, and we're almost talking for hours until we get all wrinkly and have to go inside.

The house is the same, but it's not the same. It's almost like all those things I wished for when I was there, I have now that I'm here. Like my shower is now kind of a walk-in and I have a separate jacuzzi bathtub, and the green couch in the kitchen is like it was when we first got it – it's totally soft and comfy and you don't sink down so far in it you can't even get up anymore, and it doesn't smell like dogs. It's awesome.

I haven't been back in my room. It makes me feel a little weird, and I haven't really wanted to sleep at all yet, so that's kind of different.

Anyhow, you did good your first time! Call me tomorrow. I love you.

>>>>

Hi, Emma. So, one thing that's helping me is Facebook. Man, I wish you could see it. So many people write on it every day, and then there are like a 100 likes for every post. Mom's gotten into it – do you believe it? She tries to answer every single post, which may sound kind of creepy, but at least she's doing something other than lying in bed and staring at the walls. So many people love you so much ...

LONG QUIET, THEN SOUND OF QUIET CRYING

Anyhow, Zack has written a few poems, and they're just beautiful ... Did you guys have a little something going on? He has the most beautiful picture of the two of you as his profile picture. I'm having a hard time looking at your pictures. You look so sassy, so full of life ...

QUIET CRYING

I'm so sorry, Emma. I can't do this right now. I love you.

>>>>

Okay, Sarah, I CAN see Facebook. Do you believe it?! I read it all the time. I'm kind of pissed I can't write back, but maybe I'll be able to figure out how to do that someday. I have been sending people songs like crazy. Some people get it right away and they think of me and they feel happy, and I feel a little jolt of energy kind of like when I'd shoot a Red Bull to try to stay awake. Some people it just kind of upsets, and I feel a little tired after that. Grandpa says I get energy and lose energy, and then he tried to explain how it all works but you know I can't understand him sometimes. Anyhow, he says I'll figure it out.

He also says I need to stop trying to spend so much time with you guys, but I'm not quite ready for that. I know, I know. I have to find some people my own age. I love Aunt Pat, but she is old and Grandpa is ancient and, anyhow, did I tell you that he doesn't actually live here? I go out to my car to ask him stuff. (Aunt Pat doesn't seem to know too much at all, but Grandpa's been here longer plus he's just so damn smart.)

So, I'm trying to get psyched to go to the high school 'cause I figure I'll find some people there. It's kind of weird. Like I was at Town House, which is where I found Aunt Pat and I didn't know anybody, but it was mostly just like Town House. I'm guessing that's what the high school will be like. I'm just not quite ready. I try to think what you would say. I think you would say something like ... "You'll know when you're ready, and you should trust yourself to know when it's right."

Thanks, Sarah! That's just what I want to hear! I don't need to push myself on this. I've got plenty of time, and I do think soon I'll get sick of just hanging out with Aunt Pat and watching repeats of seasons on DVD. My friend Ari said on Facebook that she is going to tell me everything that's happening on Vampire Diaries this season. I hope she remembers, or maybe you'll tell me.

Anyhow, hope you have a good day tomorrow. Talk soon. Love you lots!

>>>>

Hi, Emma. I just want to say that it's a good thing I have those little boys. Gus has been nicer than he's ever been in his life. I get tired so easily, and he gets really, really snuggly. And you know that's not his thing. When I cry, he keeps trying to lick my face, and I'd almost let him except, as you know, he's so good at finding – and eating – gross things on our walks.

And, of course, Charlie is just Charlie. He's hopelessly devoted and he just looks at me with his sad, sad eyes and it's like he's saying, "I'm here for you, Sarah. You know, I'd take a bullet for you if I thought it would help."

Anyhow, I'm lonelier than I've ever been, and it seems like every time I get a text or the phone rings I think for a split second, "Oh, that's Emma" and then I remember. It's amazing how intertwined with everything you are. Everything I eat makes me think of you and every blonde I see makes me think of you and every song I hear makes me think of you.

Mom is thinking of going back to London because she says she can't stand that you're everywhere, and everything makes her think of you. She thinks it's because you lived your whole life in Geneva, and I don't have the heart to tell her that you're everywhere ... and nowhere.

That's all for now. I'll call tomorrow. I love you and miss you with all my heart.

>>>>

Heeeeyyyyy. I hope Mom does go back to London. I think it would be good for her. I loved it there so much, and that means that you'll get to go back and I think it would be good for you, too. There was so much you and I still wanted to see. Maybe you can go to Paris this time and tell me all about it.

I hope that doesn't make you sad. I think someday I may get to see Paris. Grandpa says I can't because I never saw it when I was there, but I think that's crazy. If this is heaven, I ought to be able to do stuff I want to. And did I tell you that I turned into a bird when I went to my funeral? So there's that. Yep. I was a redbird and – duh – it wasn't until later when I realized that of course I was because that's Illinois State's mascot! I haven't quite been able to figure out how to do it again. But I have to believe I could go to some really awesome places as a bird.

I'll worry about Paris and birds and all that later. Right now, I'm totally into discovering everything I can do.

One thing that's awesome is that I just have to think about the food I want and, voilà, it's there. Like the other day I wanted to make popcorn but I didn't have the energy and, the next time I went past the stove, there was a pot on it and, when I took off the lid, there it was, buttered and everything. Yummy. So I went kind of crazy conjuring up all kinds of things, and I ate and ate until I thought I was going to be sick. That kind of made Aunt Pat mad because I know she knows that one of the reasons I like having her here is that she cooks really well, but I kind of think she's starting to miss her own house and she might want to go home soon.

Anyhow, after I ate all that, I weighed myself and I still weighed the same. I still kind of want to lose 10 pounds, but I'd trade if it meant I could eat anything I wanted and stay just like I am now!

Hope your diet's still going well. You were doing so great. Sarah, be tough. I know this is so, so hard for you, but you simply cannot let my leaving throw you forever. You are so strong and I love you so much, and I know you know that I always wished I could be more like you. You always know the right thing to do and say and you are so smart. Don't lose your way. Think about Mom. She needs you and I need you and I need her to be Mom and I know you can help her back to herself.

You'll find your way. I know. Give Charlie and Gus a big hug for me, and I'll give Duck a big hug for you. Love you forever. Talk tomorrow.

>>>>

So I saw my first patient today. They know I can't do the heavy stuff, so I saw someone who had "homework anxiety." Really? She seemed to be going and on and on about how anxious she was all the time and how she couldn't make herself study and how she couldn't focus. And I was like, "Oh yeah. Tell me more," but what I was saying inside was, "Are you kidding me? I lost my sister, and I'm supposed to care that you can't get it together enough to think about homework?"

The thing is, I know I should care. It's not this poor girl's fault my world is turned upside down, and I'm smart enough to know that even small stuff can seem big if it's happening to you. But I don't care, and that scares me because, if I never care again AND I don't have you anymore and my family is never the same again, what will be left of me?

On the way home, I found myself actually looking forward to telling you all about it and I wondered what you would say. I think you would say, "Sarah, you're so good at this. You'll care again someday because that's who you are and that's who you have always been, and think about all the times you had to help me get over some crazy thing that probably felt little to you."

Would you say that, Emma? God, I would give anything in the world to hear your sweet voice. I love you and miss you and hope that somewhere, somehow you can still know how much you mean to me.

>>>>

I tried not to laugh about Homework Girl, but really? I mean I can't even begin to imagine having homework anxiety. I could picture you saying all these really sweet things and be all like "are you kidding me?" inside. But the great thing is, I bet a little part of you still cared. I think we're kind of alike that way. If someone needs help, no matter how stupid it seems, you and I try to make like it's a big deal to us, too – like the time Mel was all upset because she wanted that job at the golf course and I was like "Mel, I can so see you at a golf course," even though I thought it was really dumb that she wanted that job so much. I'm sure you'll go back to Homework Girl and make her feel okay, and that's one of the things I love so much about you!

I'm totally working myself up to getting out of the house and trying to meet some people. It's a little creepy that they're all ... well ... dead, but if nothing else I'm dying to wear that pair of jeans we bought in London that so totally look like they were made just for me.

But right now Aunt Pat and I are going to go to a movie even though it seems like we're not going to be able to see any new movies. I'm really, really mad that I don't get to see the last Harry Potter. I may have to break down and actually read the books.

Talk to ya tomorrow. Love you.

>>>>

Okay, so the new phase I'm in is that I'm sad about the things you'll never get to try. Like, you will never guess what I discovered today. Salt and pepper popcorn, and it is absolutely to die for ... oops ... maybe that's the wrong phrase to use. Anyhow, you would love it 'cause it tastes kind of like those salt and pepper chips you like so much, only it's popcorn. I'm having some now in your honor.

Oh, Emma. How in the world did this happen?

SNIFFLING ... QUIET ... SOFT CRYING

I can't stand that you'll never have salt and pepper popcorn. I can't stand that you'll never get to see the new ginger app that makes everyone a red head instead of fat or old. I can't stand that you can't answer me back and make me laugh and tell me that everything is going to be okay.

I can't do this anymore tonight. I love you. I'll try to be better tomorrow.

Well, Sarah, I took your advice – or anyhow the advice I know you would given me. I went to the high school. And I have to say, it really kind of sucked.

I walked in, and the whole cafeteria was full of people. It seems like it's some kind of hang out or something, so that's good. Joey Newman was there and Donovan Wendt. Do you remember them? They were those two football players, and one of them was a senior and died when I was a freshman and one of them died when he was a freshman and I was a sophomore, so I didn't know either one all that well. But you would have thought we were best friends!

They were like "Emma!" and I was like "Joey! Donovan!" and we laughed and hugged and kind of jumped around a little bit. But even though I was really, really glad to see them and they were super glad to see me (obvi!), I could tell right away that there were lots of people I wanted to check out, especially this really cute guy that was sitting with some girl, but it didn't seem like they were "together" together.

But do you know not one person even acted like they saw me, and I know they did because I did wear the London jeans, and I'm pretty sure I looked totally hot. I was like "what's going on here?" and Joey and Donovan were like "we've been coming to the high school for years but no one talks to each other unless they knew each other before." And I'm like "well that's not going to work for me" – and so I walked right over and tried to talk to some of the other people but I got nowhere in a hurry.

I mean it was good to see Joey and Donovan and it was nice to be away from Aunt Pat for a little while, but I'm going to have to try to get some advice from Grandpa on this 'cause this is totally not what I have in mind for the rest of my life!

Anyhow, it was good to see so many people around my age, and it made me realize that I really am kind of sick of watching Friends reruns instead of having friends and just reading Facebook instead of being able to post things myself.

I'm going to keep trying to figure this out, but OMG, I so wish I could talk to you. Sorry, I'm feeling a little pissy right now, so I'm going to go try to conjure up some salt and pepper popcorn, which does sound totally awesome.

Love you.

>>>>

Hey, Emma. Today was a pretty good day. I went to the grocery store and managed to get a few things without crying while I was trying to pick between grapefruit and mangos or carrots and peas. I managed to check out without feeling the need to tell the poor clerk that my sister had died.

It's weird. There have been a couple of times when I feel like I do tonight and that is that I might be able to survive this. But then ... BAM ... something hits me out of the clear blue, and I can't breathe and I feel like my chest is being crushed again and the sun hurts my eyes and I don't want to look at anyone or *have anyone look at me. And then I wonder if I will ever be able to make it without you.*

But I get to talk about you a lot and Mom and I talk every day and Carol and I talk all the time. I even have talked with Jason more regularly. Did I tell you that he asked for one of your bells from your Christmas collection, and Mom gave him the one with the kind of bone handle that may have belonged to Grandaddy. He takes it wherever he goes and, when he misses you throughout the day, he rings it. I'm sure the people at work love that! Anyhow, it seems to bring him some comfort. You'd be shocked how hard he is taking this. But he talks about it, and so does Dad.

The one I'm most worried about is Ben. You were right that he and Alex were starting to make a "love connection" – you are such a goof – but that looks like it's not going anywhere now, and he won't talk about it. He dreads going to work because the customers ask about you all the time but he won't talk much about that either. He loves you so much and, as hard as it was for Mom and me to be away when it happened, I know it was so much harder for Dad and Ben to be there, and I just don't know if he's going to ever even be "pretend okay" again.

Well, I'm getting heavy and I don't want to, so I'll end this by letting you know that Maureen had her baby and maybe that's one of the reasons it's a good day today. Have I told you that I'm moving forward my date for my having a baby? Remember when I said that, if I wasn't married by the time I was 35, I was going to have a baby on my own? Well, now my plan is to go to Ireland on your 21st birthday and raise a Guinness in your honor and then get pregnant. No, not that night, although, maybe if I meet a good looking Irish Ginger!

But I'm going to start then and, even if I don't, it gives me something to look forward to right now.

I love you lots, baby sister. By the way, I'm going home for Dad's birthday, so I'm not going to call for a while. I'll try to figure out another way to connect with you while I'm there. I know this is going to be really, really hard for everyone. This is the first important family event that we've had since you've been gone, and I honestly can't imagine how we're going to get through it. I mean, do we go to Outback? Do we give him some presents from you? He says he doesn't want anything. He just kind of wants to get through it.

God this is hard. We're such a mess. You can come back now. There's clearly been a BIG mistake.

>>>>

Heeeeyyyyy. Thanks for the update on the family. I miss Benja so much. He doesn't ever post on Facebook, and I can't seem to connect with him to find out what's going on with him directly. Grandpa says that I need to try to stay away from certain people who will make me weak because they're having such a hard time, but I said you were having a hard time so how come we could still kind of be together? He said that you were trying so hard and that your feelings weren't all mixed up. He said that you were mostly just sad, and sad was okay because it IS sad and there's no getting around it.

I asked him about the high school, and he got kind of mad at me and told me that I should make do with Donovan and Joey for now and that not hanging out with the others was "one of the rules." When I asked what rule, he said that I couldn't experience certain things that I hadn't on earth and one of those was get to get real close with people I didn't know. I told him about Elmer and all the old people at Town House, and he said *that of course I had "experienced" waiters I didn't know and I wanted to say, "Oh please." Sounds like some of this is just kind of convenient, but I'm too tired of thinking hard to figure it out right now.*

I'm feeling really bad about Dad's birthday, too. I'm so glad we made a big deal for him last year, and I really outdid myself for Father's Day so there's that. It's so weird that we spent so much on the "you are my sunshine" art for Christmas. As I look back, I wonder if maybe somehow in the very, very core of me, I knew that it would be my last.

Okay, now I'm really getting sad. And on top of all that I can't seem to make salt and pepper popcorn. I keep trying but all I get is kettle corn. I even went to the store to try to make it the old fashioned way, but I couldn't find it anywhere.

Whine, whine, whine, right? Oh, well. I love you and I miss you and we'll talk soon.

$>>>>$

Hi, Emma. I'm back from Geneva and I'm really sorry ... SNIFFLING, SILENCE ... *Emma, I just can't do this anymore. It turns out it's not helping me. I mean it feels good to talk to you but, really, it's not real, and I prove that it isn't real every time I say something and you don't say something back. It's just too hard. I'm starting to forget what you sound like, and it's just way too painful to keep putting myself into situations where I am so exposed to the pain of not having you.*

Maybe I can do this again someday, but I need to hear your voice someplace other than my head. I can't keep doing this. I am just so sad. I thought I was kind of making progress, but then I was just standing there last night doing the dishes — doing the dishes of all things. And I started to sob and I couldn't catch my breath. I cried for hours. I think the only reason I stopped was because I was so exhausted I finally fell asleep.

I just can't do it. I love you. I miss you. I just can't stand that you're never, never on the other end of my words.

Sarah, don't give up. I need to talk with you. You help me so much. I pretend you're listening and giving me advice. I need you. Don't leave me. Sarah, what can I do to make you stay? Sarah, please, please stay ...

Emma

Chapter 19

Emma sat at the table for a long time, staring at Sarah's picture. Finally, she finished her wine and blew out the candle. *Okay,* she thought, *it's time to figure this out ... I want Sarah back, and I'm going to get her back.* She grabbed a Red Bull, a notebook, and a pen and started to review all that she had learned so far.

What I already know	What I need to figure out
I can turn myself into something else (a bird) Some people can see me that way (Susan)	Are there other things I can turn into? How did I do it? Why can some people see me and others can't?
I can go places by car or by some other way ("transporting?")	What was going on when I got from Town House to the hospital with my dad?
I can see and hear people They can't see and hear me	How come I can't do this all the time?
I can still see Facebook posts I can't post	How come I can still see new posts? Is there a way to post back?
I can be with dead people who I knew before I can be with dead people I didn't know before but I can't make friends with them	How can I make new friends with new people?

| I made my dad hear me once | What was going on when that happened with him? What was going on when that happened with me? |
| I can send music and people can hear it | How come only some people know it's from me? How come it makes some people feel good and others feel terrible? |

Emma paused. *Think as hard as you have ever thought,* she encouraged herself. *Is there anything else that you know?* After a few minutes she started to write again.

| I can't see new movies or TV shows I can keep up with them if someone posts stuff on Facebook | Can I use Facebook to find stuff I need to find? |
| I am energized by good things that happen on earth and drained by bad things | Can I somehow control this? Can I influence this? |

Emma studied her list. *Okay,* she said. *Now look at this and ask yourself, how can this help me figure out how to get Sarah back?*

The easiest thing to do, she knew, would be to ask Grandpa. But Grandpa seemed like he really didn't want her to spend all of her time with her family and friends. He also – and this made no sense to her – didn't seem to really want her to make new friends. He suggested that she find more people she knew before they died, but she was only 19, and she didn't really know that many people who are dead now. No, her very best friend was Sarah − Sarah was what she needed right now.

She doodled on her list for a while.

Things that can help me:
 IPhone
 Facebook
 Music
 Birds
 Apps???

Are there any apps that might help? she wondered. Ben had turned her on to StumbleUpon recently, and she loved it. *I wonder if there's anything about "connecting" or "spirits."* (It was still so weird to think about herself as a "spirit.") She searched the categories and decided maybe "paranormal," "goth culture," and "spirituality" would pull up something of interest. She skimmed through the results, and nothing really popped out, though she did find a few things to read later and saved the categories as personal interests.

Since there didn't seem to be any kind of app shortcut, she went out to the internet and googled "communicating with the living." She got a bunch of self-help stuff about how you should live life to the fullest, and this confused her at first, but then ... *Duh!* ... she realized that she would have to figure this out from Sarah's perspective because apparently the internet wasn't designed to be directly helpful to dead people!

So, she entered "communicating with the dead" and got a number of extremely helpful hits. She was particularly intrigued with entries about a guy named Edgar who had been some kind of famous, and apparently really good, psychic. He founded something called the Association for Research and Enlightenment. She made a note that he died in 1945 in case she could figure out a way to "conjure" him up later. He had been an expert on dream visits and she remembered that Doni told her about her dad visiting in her dream one time so she knew it could happen. Apparently, dreams were good connecting opportunities because, when people were asleep, they were in a "subconscious state" and more open to things that might normally freak them out. Like visits from dead people.

She made a note that it was easier if the living person: 1) wanted to make contact (Sarah clearly wanted to talk to her – she stopped only because Emma wasn't talking back) and 2) was listening hard enough.

This second part was interesting. Apparently Sarah would be more open to a dream visit if she was feeling peaceful and if a bunch of things that reminded her of Emma hit her all at once. That would open up her "listening" channels. Emma added an entry to her list of what she knew.

People associate stars, shining, sunflowers, and red birds (kind of) with me

Emma jotted down the beginnings of a plan:

1. Keep watching Sarah, particularly when she is getting ready for bed

That seemed to be the time when Sarah's defenses were already down and she allowed herself to think about Emma the most. Come to think of it, Emma noticed that it was times that Sarah was thinking about her the most that were the same times she could see Sarah the clearest. She made a note in her ever-growing "what I know" column and continued with her plan.

2. Listen for clues for when Sarah is feeling peaceful or at least mellow

3. When #2 happens, send a bunch of "Emma" songs or other Emma signs that would make Sarah think about me harder

4. When conditions feel right, focus all my energy on being with Sarah

... just like she had with her dad right before she found him in the hospital.

After a few minutes she also added:

5. It would be extremely helpful if I could find a way to get her to read about Edgar!!

It probably wasn't the best plan in the world, but it was a start.

Just as she finished with it, her stomach growled and she realized she had been working for a while. After checking her Facebook (*Hey Kevin, hey Zack. Oh my gosh, I miss you, too, Alexa. I wasn't actually there when you talked the cop out of the speeding ticket, but maybe I could have been! And it was so, so sweet of you to think it was me. Love you!*), she decided she would take a break and go to McDonald's to grab a bite to eat.

She took a final look at her lists and pushed herself one last time. After a few minutes of just letting her thoughts go, she realized that she hadn't really noted the biggest questions of all.

Where am I? Is this heaven? If it is heaven, is there a ... is there a God? If there is a God, can he ... well of course he <u>can</u>, she corrected herself ... *<u>will</u> he help me get Sarah back?* If God would help, that would definitely go in the plus column and increase her odds!

There was a huge church near the McDonald's right by her house and she decided that, if she were going to get answers to questions like this, it made sense that she go there after lunch and see what she could find out.

She parked her car in the church parking and sat for a while eating her lunch and trying to figure out a few more details about how she might find God. Nothing really came to her so she decided this would be a "wing it" moment.

She got out of the car and tried the front door. She didn't really expect it to be open – *I may have to kamikaze through the window as a bird,* she thought – but it was, and she walked right in.

She walked around a little and didn't see anyone. *God?* she called out tentatively and felt kind of ridiculous for doing so. She explored the Sunday School classrooms and leafed through the religious booklets, but nothing came to her. She checked in the offices and even the bathrooms, periodically calling out, *Hey, God,* but she got no response. Finally, she went into the sanctuary, sat down in the pew, held a Bible to her chest, and stared at the cross.

She could kind of feel herself going into a little bit of a trance from concentrating so hard, but nothing much happened.

After a while, just as she was about to give up, she heard a tentative voice call her name. She was way more nervous than she ever anticipated, and she found herself thinking that she probably should have changed into something a little more conservative.

Is this it? Am I about to come face-to-face with God? And she wondered how long would be an appropriate amount of time before she asked him for a favor?

She turned ...

... and there, standing behind her was not God ...

... but Sammy Cook, who was 13 years old when he died. In fact, she attended his funeral in this very church.

~

It had been a life-changing experience for her. Even though she hadn't known Sammy very well, she was horrified by his death. It was the first time it entered her consciousness that a kid could actually die. There had been something wrong with him, but she never really knew what. He had some kind of seizures all the time, so a lot of kids kept their distance and he didn't have a lot of friends. She knew him because she sat next to him in homeroom, and he was a really nice kid.

His funeral was on a Wednesday on a hot summer day. She remembered this vividly because she insisted that her mom take time off from work to take her. Mom protested initially because it meant she'd have to take a whole vacation day off from work (and she hadn't known Sammy at all) but, in the end, she agreed as Emma knew she would.

Her friend Gina wanted to go as well, so they picked her up on the way, and they arrived at the church and parked in a spot that she now realized was very close to where she parked today. They were surprised that there were so few cars and, when they made their way into the sanctuary, they realized why. There was practically no one there! Oh, Sammy's parents and family were there in the front pews quietly crying but, besides them, there were maybe 20 other people scattered around, and that was it.

They were horrified. Emma kept expecting more people to show up, but no one did. As soon as the service was over, Sammy's family left through the front door, but Emma and Gina and Mom continued to sit there, even after the minister led the others into the reception hall. They felt that something had gone completely awry in the universe.

How does a little boy die, Mom asked incredulously, *and no one takes time out of their day to show him that he mattered?* Emma couldn't help but think now about the difference between that funeral and her own, also on a weekday on a hot summer day.

~

God, I am lucky, she thought to herself as she said, *Sammy!* out loud and went to give him a big hug. *How the heck are you, kiddo?* she asked, and she was a little uncomfortable at the way he seemed to be gazing adoringly at her.

Well, I've been kind of lonely. I mean my grandma is here and I live with her, but I don't really have too many friends, he admitted. In fact, he went on, *I really don't have any. Apparently there's some kind of rule ...*

Yeah, I know all about that, said Emma, *and I'm trying to figure out how to fix it! Why are you here?*

Well, I was a pretty good kid, so I guess I got to come here.

No, no, no, Emma broke in. *I mean at the church.*

Oh, this was my church, Sammy said, *and I had some of my best times here. Even though there's no one to play with, I still like it here. Sometimes I shoot hoops on the basketball court, and sometimes I read in the library and, you know, just kind of hang out.*

Once again, Emma's heart was breaking for this kid she barely knew. *Why don't you come home with me for a while – here, you can use my phone to call your grandma,* she said automatically and then realized with a start that he, in fact, <u>could</u> use her phone to call his Grandma. *(Add that to my list,* she thought to herself.) *And we can play some two-people games if you want.*

Sammy was beside himself and puffed out his chest with pride when he got in next to her in her car. *By the way,* Emma asked as she pulled out of the parking lot, *have you ever run into God in there*? And, when he responded that he hadn't, she sighed a little. *That would have been way too easy,* she decided and found that she was ridiculously happy that she was the one who was there for Sammy. *Imagine that,* she thought. *Being excited to have a 13-year-old to hang out with,* and with a little

laugh she asked what game he'd most missed playing so
that they could do that first when they got to her house.

Sarah

Chapter 20

Hi, Ben. I had to call someone right away, and Mom is at work ... You're not going to believe this ... Emma came to me in a dream, and I really think it was her. I really felt her presence ...

Dad and you and I were on a cruise ship and we were trying to decide whether to take a trip or not and I was getting really excited about it. I said, "Since Emma died, I just want to ex-perience absolutely everything I can," but you guys weren't getting it at all ... You were kind of making fun of me and saying there's no way we should go away, especially so soon after Emma died. Then you and Dad walked away one way, and I kind of huffed away the other and I turned the corner ... and there she was ...

She walked right up to me and I said, "Oh, my gosh, Emma," and I knew she was dead and she knew she was dead, but she just smiled and started to walk with me ... It was as natural as if I had just seen her the day before. She asked me how I was doing with my diet and I said, "Well I gained a lot of weight when you died, but it seems like I'm back on track now." She was really happy about that and said that she was so proud of me and that it was so important for me to be healthy ... I asked if she was doing okay, and she said she had been kind of moody and homesick at first, kind of like she was when she went to college. Just like her first semester, there were times when she was doing okay ... even having fun. But she definitely still missed all of us and her old friends ...

She said she was sorry about Matt, and I wish I asked her how she knew about that. I couldn't think of all the things I wanted to say to her, but that was okay. It just felt right to be with her again. She seemed so peaceful and ... I don't know ... kind of "grounded" ...

We just walked together for a while and after a few minutes we turned another corner, and we saw Kevin standing with some people I didn't know. Emma said that she had to go talk with him and I said, "Wait, don't go, this is my dream," and she kind of squeezed my hand and said, "No, he needs me more than you do right now ..." She promised we'd talk again real soon ...

Even though she wasn't near me anymore, I could still hear everything she was saying to Kevin. She told him that she was concerned about how he was living. She was so calm and totally non-judgmental. You could tell how much she loved him and just wanted to help ease his pain ... She said that he needed to get himself a new outlook, that he should "flash forward" rather than live his life in the past. She said that's how she lived her life so, when she died and her aunt asked her if she needed a hug, she realized that was the <u>only</u> thing she needed ...

I started to cry and became kind of restless, and I ended up waking myself up even though all I wanted to do was stay with her ... Gus and Charlie were clearly trying to comfort me, so I guess I had been crying for a while. But the dream wasn't sad. I was just sad because I couldn't be with Emma anymore ...

I heard her as clear as a bell. She spoke to me, and I heard her voice. I have missed that so much ... I told her I needed to hear her voice a few days ago, and last night she was there. She really was. I know I keep trying to find things that can be "substitute Emmas," but this really truly was Emma ...

I'm not sure what I did different last night than any other night. Of course, I jumped on Google right away to see what it all meant, and there's this guy named Edgar Cayce who was a huge dream expert. He started the Association for Research and Enlightenment. One of the things it said was that, if there is a two-way dialog in a dream, it is very likely that it is a real visit, that your subconscious has connected with the bodiless consciousness of your loved one. I know that may be just something I want to believe but, Ben, I do believe it ...

I want you to have that same experience ... I think it would really help you ... I know you're having a really hard time sleeping, but I read that you could try to ask Emma to come and talk with you before you fall asleep. That might help ...

Oh, Ben. I'm telling you it was real, and I really want her to come and visit you, too ... I love you, and I'm worried about you ... You'll call me or talk to Mom if it gets too bad, right? I almost feel like I'm losing you, too, and I can't – I won't – let that happen ... Will you do it for me? Will you ask Emma to come and visit you? ... Promise?

Patsy

Nailed it, Emma sang out as she came skipping into the family room. *I am a rock star!*

Patsy put down the book she was reading and laughed. *What now?* she said in anticipation. Emma was definitely getting more animated by the day, and right now she was smiling like a Cheshire cat.

You know the plan I told you about to get Sarah to keep talking to me? Well, it didn't really work the way I planned, but ... – and Emma did a little dance around the room – *I did it. I figured out how to talk to Sarah.*

Do tell, Patsy said and couldn't help getting caught up in Emma's excitement. She herself had never tried to connect with her kids or her sister, and she found herself daring to hope that she might learn something that could help her spend some time doing something other than just watching them.

Well, my mom helped out without even realizing it. After she went back to London, she and Sarah were having a hard time figuring out a time they could facetime. Apparently a few weeks ago, Mom told Sarah that she could have my phone since it's the only one with FaceTime, and she and Dad went to the Apple store and had it switched over to Sarah's number. I have zero idea how all of this works – I've written some more questions on my list – but thankfully I still have my phone, too ... maybe 'cause my dad downloaded everything off my phone to his computer.

Anyhow, that's not important. What is important is that I could make my phone – that phone, the one Sarah now has – do what I wanted it to. Believe me, no one knows that phone better than I do.

So, you remember that Step 3 of my plan was to send Sarah things that would make her think of me, and I was worried 'cause I don't know how to do that except with songs. And then, voilà, Mom puts it right in her hands. The thing that would make her think most about me almost more than anything else ... my phone. It was absolutely perfect.

Patsy was so proud of Emma. She was definitely settling in nicely. *Soon,* she thought, *she won't really need me with her all the time,* and she realized with a pang that that would be a very, very sad day for her.

Emma went on, *I immediately started making my phone hang up every time Sarah tried to use it.*

Well, that makes sense, Patsy said, but Emma missed the sarcasm.

I know, right? Well, it didn't work. Sarah got an app to fix that. Then I really got smart. You know the camera light on an iPhone? I made it shine ... shine, get it? Then all I had to do was wait until she went to bed and took her phone, which she always does 'cause she plays a last round of Words with Friends. Of course, it shone brighter in the dark, and she actually said, "Emma, are you trying to tell me something?" and I was beside myself!!

She finally fell asleep thinking of me, and then it was easy. I just closed my eyes and thought about one of my very favorite vacations I ever had with her and – bam – there I was, walking right next to her on a cruise ship. OMG, it was Emm-azing!!

Better than songs really 'cause I talked to her, and she answered me. It was like a regular conversation.

You are something else, Patsy agreed. *Just look at you. You said you were going to do it, and by golly you figured it out. How long did you talk with her?*

Well, there was a little bit of a problem that I didn't expect, Emma said a little sheepishly. *Somehow, I got a two-fer ... I channeled into Kevin at the same time. I have absolutely no idea how that happened. But he is so sad. He misses me so much and I know Sarah does, too, but this was the first time I got to see Kevin, and so I kind of excused myself from Sarah and went to spend some time with him.*

Who's Kevin again? Pat asked.

Oh, he's my very best friend. (And Pat laughed to herself as she wondered not for the first time how many very best friends Emma actually had.) *I love him so much. I was a little disappointed when he figured out he was gay 'cause I thought we might hook up someday, but he turned out to be way better as a best friend than I think he would ever have been as a boyfriend. Anyhow, he's feeling really bad, and I knew I could help him. His posts have been really sad and he's usually so funny and I want to help him be funny again. So I talked to him, too, and I really think I made him feel better. I can't wait to see what he posts tonight.*

I'm sure you made him feel better and Sarah, too, Patsy said. *I don't know if this place knows what's hit it quite yet! You know it hasn't been that long, and just look at what you've accomplished.*

Emma practically glowed with pride. *The only problem is, I am completely exhausted. I'm starting to understand this energy drain and energy gain stuff that Grandpa talked about. So, I'm going to go relax in the hot tub for a few. Do you want to come?*

No, I'm at a really good spot in my book.

Okay. After the hot tub, I'm going to work on visiting my brother. I haven't been able to see him very well, and he doesn't talk out loud very much. I miss him so much. I can't wait to talk to him. Still beaming, Emma gave Patsy a quick kiss on the cheek and danced out of the room.

As Emma breezed out, her energy and happiness swished out behind her, and even the room felt her loss. *God, I'm going to miss her,* Patsy thought and, with a sigh, she picked up her book.

Ben

Ben was an absolute wreck. He was an introvert by nature and would have greatly preferred to get through life without talking to anyone except occasionally a few close friends, his family, and Duck (before he died). Now it seemed that everyone wanted to talk with him every minute of every day about things so deep that there were no words to express them, even for people who wanted to talk all the time, like his Mom.

Ben, are you sure you're okay, she'd ask over and over again. Every conversation with Sarah started out that she was worried about him. Even Dad seemed to want to talk about how he was doing.

The people at work had learned not to say too much, but he knew they were thinking about Emma all the time. He could feel their pity and, though he knew it came from a good place, it made him almost physically ill to try to act like everything was okay every second of every waking minute of every single day. On top of that, so often when he looked at Vicki and Doug and Jill, he relived that terrible day when he returned from the hospital to say the dreaded words out loud, *She didn't make it. Emma's gone.*

And the customers? So many of them had known Emma, and it seemed like everyone wanted to know how he and the family were doing. Again, well-intentioned, but he wondered how in the world was he supposed to concentrate on remembering the daily soups and desserts, taking orders and keeping straight which person got which sandwich when any minute someone might cut through the armor he had worked hard to build by saying something amazingly stupid like, *I bet you're really sad* (Are you kidding me?) or *How is your Mom holding up?* (Oh, she's still not able to breathe, thanks for asking) or *We really miss Emma* (Do you? I kind of miss her, too).

In fairness, they were all trying. No one knew what to say and, in a weird way, you had to kind of admire the people who tried. The worst situations by far were the people who hadn't heard – *So, Ben, how is Emma enjoying her sophomore year?* – or even worse, the people who didn't know Emma and had heard something but not much and didn't realize that their words would be like sharpened daggers to him. *Hey, we heard someone from Town House died. What happened? Thank goodness it wasn't Doug or Vicki.* Insert knife into heart, twist, take out, insert again.

He had definitely given everything he had at the funeral. When he thought back to that day (and God, he tried so hard not to), he couldn't imagine that it was really he who stood up in front of all those people and poured his heart out. Perhaps he was still recovering from the effort that had taken.

But now ... *Be done,* he said in his head to everyone who wanted to keep talking. He almost wished he could hand out transcripts of his eulogy. *You want to know how I am? You want to know how much I miss my sister? Here, read this.* Or, alternatively, he occasionally envisioned himself one day answering those inane questions by telling people exactly how he felt and, as the look of horror on their faces grew, pausing and saying dramatically, *Oh, I'm sorry. Did you not really want to know?* It had been done before, he knew (think Bill Murray in *Groundhog Day* answering the poor innkeeper who asked about the weather), but perhaps it would help his anger subside, albeit momentarily and at the expense of being less than polite.

So, yes, he was a mess. Every day at work required so much energy that it was like walking through molasses, and he just wasn't sleeping well at night. For several days after Emma died, he would fall asleep exhausted around midnight and then startle awake at exactly 4:04. He was convinced now that this was the time that she died. Some people would probably think that was kind of cool because they'd think Emma was trying to connect with him or some other kind of voices-from-the-dead crap. But for him, it was just unnerving. And then of course he couldn't go back to sleep.

Once in a while in the dark of the night he would try to talk with her. To make Sarah happy, he even asked Emma to come and talk to him.

Man, had that backfired. She was talking to him alright. Recently, for several nights in a row, she appeared in his dream all perky and sassy and trying to convince him she was okay ... that this had all been some kind of terrible mistake. She would come up with elaborate stories about what she had been doing this whole time, and he would keep pushing back saying, *Emma stop talking crazy. You're dead and you're going to stay dead and we all know that.*

But she would work on him and work on him just like she did when she was alive when she wanted something big time and all of his instincts told him that what she wanted was not going to turn out well. And, just like when that had happened, he would finally give in. Finally, in his dream, he would believe her. Happiness would spread through him like a wildfire, and he would feel whole again.

He'd start to imagine what it would be like when he told his family that Emma was okay. He could picture the pure joy that would envelop them when she stepped back into their lives as though she had never left. The grief and exhaustion would wash away, and their lives would again be filled with light and laughter ...

... and then he'd wake up. Reality would set in and, though he wouldn't have thought it possible, his heart would be even heavier than it had been the night before. If it got too much heavier, he wouldn't be able to get out of bed in the morning and then his Mom would realize that *I'm okay* was just a sham. What would happen to her if she knew that he was close to losing his way and that some days he actually hoped that his life would just blink out so that he wouldn't have to feel this overwhelming weight?

He tried to stop sleeping at all in an attempt to stave off the dream. That, of course, didn't work. But, blessedly, just when he thought he couldn't take one more night, Emma stopped coming. And then ... now this was really sick ... he was almost sorry. Because, in truth, those few minutes between when she had finally convinced him everything was going to be okay and when he woke up ... those few minutes were the happiest he felt since she had been gone. So, despite how excruciating that roller coaster ride had been, he almost didn't want it to end. It seemed any Emma might be better than no Emma.

Then there was Alex. All his life he had wanted to date ... okay, say it out loud ... to *love* someone like Alex. Alex and Emma had become friends at Town House while Ben was in California. Emma referred to Alex frequently when she told Town House stories and, after Ben came back from California, he felt he already knew her and what a great girl she was. Apparently, Emma had told Alex some Ben stories because she seemed to like him right away, too, and they slipped into an easy friendship. Right before she went to London, Emma told him that he should wake up and notice that he had a shot with Alex and, once Ben started to really pay attention, it did seem that her hand lingered on his when she handed him wine to take to his customers and that she laughed pretty hard at his jokes.

In the few days that Emma worked after she came back from London, she picked up where she had left off and even ratcheted up her campaign to get Alex and Ben together by teasing him mercilessly that, if he played his cards right, he was about to get *very, very lucky.*

Not everyone was so supportive. Although neither Alex nor Ben openly acknowledged their growing attraction, even to each other, speculation that something was in the air ran rampant. The other female servers were even getting a little snooty. Alex was older than Ben and ... divorced ... and so their protective instincts came out in spades. Despite her private teasing, when other servers said that he was headed for a fall, Emma defended him like a mother bird defends her chicks. *I told them you deserve to be happy and, if they truly wanted what was best for you, they should just back the hell off,* she reported back to Ben and, even though he hadn't yet fessed up that he was falling for Alex, he was on the brink of making Emma the first person to know. He was about to let himself say the words out loud.

And then she died. She died. Emma is dead. He still had to say it over and over again because he still couldn't quite wrap his head around it. And then Emma died, and now she would never know that he had almost been happy.

And so, he turned his back on Alex. He worked hard to turn off any feelings he had for her because he knew that he could not allow happiness into his life. That would not be consistent with Emma being dead, and Ben was committed to some semblance of consistency and calm and balance. Emma was dead. Ergo: Ben should not be happy. Ergo: Alex was a dream that could never become a reality.

The thing was, Alex would not turn her back on Ben. And he had to work with her two days a week. And those two days were even harder than all the others because, when he accidentally looked at Alex, he saw color and felt warmth and that was not right. His world was gray and cold now, and gray and cold it decidedly needed to stay. For Emma. He simply could not be happy when Emma would never be happy – would never be *anything* – ever again.

So he tried to keep not looking at Alex, and he politely answered, *I'm fine,* when customers asked how he was doing, and he worked harder to get through each day and to try to sleep through each night. And he privately worried that he was so lost, he may never be able to find his way again.

Emma

Emma's heart was breaking. What had she done to Ben? Grandpa Mebane had been right. She was playing with something she didn't understand, and now she had made things worse for her brother.

She had been so sure that she could make him understand that she was okay. Now she had to add that "dream visits could really backfire" to her growing list of things she knew. She should have remembered that dreams were often confusing, and she should have realized that she might not be able to make Ben understand what she was trying to tell him.

But she had made contact. *That was the important thing,* she reminded herself. She wouldn't visit him again until she knew she could figure out how to make him understand, how to comfort him and help him find his way. But she would figure it out! Connecting with Sarah – making something happen because she wanted to make it happen – was a real boost to her confidence, and she had no doubt that she was going to make this work for her whole family.

As she reflected back over the time she had been here, she believed that she had made real progress. Oh, she knew there was much more to learn. And, she realized with a start, she actually was kind of looking forward to learning it. *This is turning into a bit of an adventure,* she thought to herself. Now that she knew Sarah could still be her touchpoint, much like she had been on earth, Emma felt a certain freedom to begin exploring her new life in earnest.

Her dad seemed to be doing okay – Emma had been kind of messy, and it seemed to help him that there was still so much of her to sort through and organize. She smiled to herself that his publishing her *A Book Abot Chaps* could be just the beginning of a long partnership between them. After all, she had drawn it way back in the first grade, before she even knew how to spell the word for "shapes" (chaps) or "square" (skwar) or "diamond" (dimind). He had boxes and boxes saved of all her projects that he still had to sort through. She may just become known as an artist, with Dad by her side. She may even be a published writer someday. The latest post to Facebook was a poem she had written about Juice that Dad had uncovered in his box of special treasures.

Pet Love

Orange ball of fuzz
Sleeping on my bed
Dancing green eyes and a cold wet nose
With a very soft purr
Which makes my lap vibrate as I hold him
Even at age 5, I knew love

by Emma Mebane

Yes, her dad was going to be okay in time. Her mom was still a worry and, man, how Emma missed her. But figuring out how to connect with her would have to wait. Her mom was graduate school material. She would have to work her way up to Mom once she had things down

pat with others. She couldn't let herself think about her
too much just yet. But, if this was the afterlife (and, really,
what else could it be?), she had an eternity to figure out
what to do. She knew that this was the toughest thing her
mom would ever have to face, and she took full respon-
sibility – even though, really, it hadn't been her fault.
Still, she knew it was up to her to make it right, but right
now she needed all of her strength.

Her friends seemed to be regaining their balance a
little. More and more of them seemed to understand that
it was she who was sending them songs, and the posts on
her Wall, though still heavily weighted toward missing
her, were starting to include past posts she had made to
them and memories of all of their best times together. So,
it was like a really good movie that makes you laugh and
cry all at the same time.

Yes, everything seemed to be mostly under control in
her old life. It was time, then, to apply herself to making
friends here. She went to the high school every day during the lunch hour and hung out with Donovan and Joey,
which was fun for sure. But her real motive was to try to
figure out who the pretty girl and the hot guy were who
always sat next to each other. She walked past them
several times, pretending to get water from the water
fountain, and she finally overheard enough to piece
together their names. The girl was Alice Watson, and the
guy was Flynn Thomas. *Flynn – now there was a movie star
name if ever there was one.*

While she was on Facebook with her BEFORE friends,
she hatched an idea that she was pretty sure was going to

work. However, she didn't want to try it out on Flynn first just in case it didn't. Alice would be her practice run.

The plan was pretty simple, really. Grandpa had said she couldn't make friends with people she hadn't known on earth. But what if she *practically* had known them on earth? What if they had been *almost* connected and had just never taken that last step that would have brought them into the same orbit? What if that last step was meant to be made here, in this AFTER Geneva? What if they were like 5 degrees of Kevin Bacon BEFORE and she could make the 6th one happen now that they were both living in AFTER?

Once she came up with this concept, she set to work on Facebook. She made the assumption that Alice died in Illinois – otherwise she wouldn't be at this high school (which, she recently learned, was the designated teen meeting place for northern Illinois). It didn't take her long to find the right Alice Watson – there were three in the state and one of them had grandchildren and one of them was black. That left <u>her</u> Alice and, once she opened her profile (which had a profile picture of Kermit the Frog instead of Alice just to make it a little challenging), she knew she had found the right one. Her information didn't specifically say she had died, but then Emma's didn't either.

Emma realized that Alice's profile wasn't completely private, which was a bit of good luck. So, Emma quickly learned that they both loved the movie *The Notebook* and the TV show *It's Always Sunny in Philadelphia* and that they were both Damen (vs. Stefan) fans for *Vampire Diaries* and neither one of them had political views. But

Emma knew that wasn't enough to really know someone. Anyone looking could find that out. She had to dig a little deeper.

Emma could see immediately that they had no friends in common, but she looked through all of them anyhow, just in case. Although there were a few whose name sounded familiar, she finally conceded that she didn't know any of them. *That would have been too easy.* So she began to search on friends of Alice's relatives. And there she got very, very lucky! Her sister, Sally, went to ISU and was in the dance club. Emma knew her best friend, Taylor, had a sister, Kelsey, who was into dance while she was at ISU and – *Bingo!* They had been in the same dance club! Emma searched Kelsey's friends and sang out with joy when she saw that Kelsey and Sally were Facebook friends.

From there it was easy since, fortunately, after Kelsey had her baby, Emma had friended her so she could see absolutely every picture of that adorable baby boy. Emma was able to learn just about everything there was to know about Alice through Sally (via Kelsey) because, of course, Sally was friends with Alice.

She laughed at Alice's antics with her friends – so much like her own. She cried when she read about her death, just a year before Emma's. For the first few months after Alice died, Sally's posts were filled with sadness and then they slowly tapered off altogether. *(God, how I hope Sarah keeps posting,* Emma thought.) Emma kind of lost the plot after that. Still, she felt like she really knew Alice and, after a few practice runs with Patsy about what she would say to win her over, Emma was ready.

She dressed in her London jeans and put on a sophisticated blue top that she felt made her look smart. (Alice had been an honors student.) She put her hair in a ponytail because that's how Alice wore hers. She grabbed her DVD of *The Notebook* and stopped at Graham's Chocolate along the way to get a box of pecan turtles because they were Alice's favorite food, and Graham's had the very best candy in the whole world. She thought about getting some daisies (Alice's favorite flower) but decided that might be a little over the top.

Emma parked her car and walked slowly into the cafeteria trying to calm her nerves. *This just has to work,* she thought. *I didn't ask for all this, and I'm trying to make the best of it. So, can someone just please, please cut me a break?*

She took a deep breath, walked right past Joey and Donovan and stood in front of Alice's table. She cleared her throat and started to sing:

> *Day man, oooh ahh ahh*
> *Fighter of the night man, oooh ahh ahh*
> *Champion of the sun, oooh ahh ahh*
> *You're a master of karate*
> *And friendship for everyone*

Emma went into a karate chop stance. *Okay, you can do this Emma,* she said to herself as she noted that not only did she have Alice's attention, but just about everyone else had stopped what they were doing to look at her.

Charlie, right? He's my favorite character in "It's Always Sunny." How about you? Charlie, right? What's not to love about Charlie? and, before she lost her momentum, she

moved right into a soliloquy about why Damon was
better for Elena on *Vampire Diaries* even though he was
such a bad boy. Mostly her argument boiled down to that
Stephan was just a little too nice and, really, Damon was
just so hot. Alice hid her mouth behind her hand, and
Emma thought she detected a little smile. Encouraged,
Emma went on.

*The thing is, Alice, we're a lot alike, you and I. I never
really had a boyfriend and, if you don't count that creeper
James who made out with your friend during the freshman
dance – and really he seemed so not right for you – you didn't
either, and I totally understand how you can love your best
friends even though you're secretly jealous 'cause they are all
starting to have boyfriends and you don't. And I worried, too,
that my best friends – Carrie and Paige and Taylor – were
going to stop wanting to hang out with me 'cause, even though
they pretended they didn't want to be with their boyfriends all
the time, let's get real ... They probably did. And my sister is
totally my best friend, too, just like Sally is yours. By the way,
do you know how to visit her in dreams? 'Cause I do, and I can
teach you. I'm sure she misses you all the time, and I know how
hard it must be for you.*

*I saw you like cats better than dogs – me, too! I saw you
wanted to be a teacher – me, too! But then I didn't because I
started worrying maybe I wasn't smart enough. You seem like
you're real smart, though, and I think you would have made a
great teacher. I think we would have been good friends if we
had met before. We have so many things in common. But the
biggest reason I feel like I already know you? We both picked a
line from the Heart of Life by John Mayer for our senior quote.*

Emma paused and took another deep breath. She could feel all eyes on her. Fortunately, this was the part she had practiced the most. It was one of her all time favorite songs. Her family played it at her funeral, and she put every ounce of feeling she had into it. Her voice sang out, simple and pure, and with just the right balance of hurt and hope.

> *Pain throws your heart to the ground*
> *Love turns the whole thing around*
> *No it won't all go the way it should*
> *But I know the heart of life is good*

When she was through, the silence around her was absolute. She picked up the box of chocolates and set them down in front of Alice along with *The Notebook* DVD.

You could come to my house later, she said, and there was gentle pleading in her voice. *We could watch this movie and eat pecan turtles. I could make popcorn – I make the best popcorn. Please, Alice. Couldn't you really use a girl-friend?*

Emma held her breath. She had worked hard for this, and she had given it her best shot. She had no idea what she would do next if this didn't work.

Alice didn't say a word. Her head was bowed a little, and she still had the back of her hand up over her mouth. After what seemed like several minutes, her shoulders started to shake. *Uh-oh*, Emma thought. *Maybe I messed up like I did with Ben. Maybe I just made her sad ...*

... but no. Alice finally looked up at Emma and ... was she really? ... OMG, she was laughing. She was laughing right out loud. Pretty soon Emma heard another hearty laugh, and she recognized the deep baritone of Joey Newman, then Donovan, and before she knew it everybody else joined in, too. Emma looked right into Alice's eyes, gave a little shrug, and started to laugh a little herself.

Hi, Emma, Alice said, as she stood and pulled her into a hug. *It's really nice to meet you.*

Grandpa

Chapter 24

Grandpa Mebane sat in Emma's car and watched her hug her new friend goodbye at the door of the cafeteria before she skipped across the parking lot. He didn't know whether to be angry, worried, or proud. She had clearly, deliberately, and with full intent broken a deeply rooted rule.

He knew she understood it when he explained it to her. So, yes, he was angry. He wasn't sure what happened when rules were broken ... To his knowledge it hadn't ever happened or, if it had, not as publicly as Emma had just done it. He wasn't sure what would happen. He loved Emma and didn't want her to be hurt in any way. So, yes, he was more than a little worried.

But on the other hand, *Lord, is she a character!* He considered himself one who pushed the rules a bit on earth, and so there was a part of him that reveled in the fact that she had a solid Mebane streak in her. *I think she might have gotten that from me,* he theorized now and, really, how could that not make him just a little bit proud?

Here she comes, he thought to himself. *I better start with angry.*

Grandpa Mebane watched as Emma saw him and pulled up short. *Good, she is nervous. At least she realizes she did something wrong.* If he knew Emma, though, and he was pretty sure he did, she would go on the offensive immediately. Hadn't he taught her himself during one of their many chats in front of a Penn State football game that sometimes the best defense was a good offense?

Heeeeyyyyy, she said as she opened the door and slipped behind the driver's seat.

Hey yourself, Grandpa replied sternly.

What ...? Emma asked and tried, but failed, for innocence.

What do you think you were doing in there?

You told me I should make friends, Emma said. (And Grandpa hid his smile that said she was doing exactly what he would have done.)

I told you, "You should have friends," and you did. You had Donovan, and Joey, and even Sammy. You haven't even connected with all the people you already knew on earth! Why in the world did you feel you had to upset the apple cart? What were you thinking?

Honestly, I wasn't trying to upset things. Donovan and Joey are fine, but I wanted a girl friend. And, Grandpa, I did know her. I knew more about her than I ever knew about Donovan and Joey. I knew her because I wanted to know her, and it was easy to find out everything about her. I liked her before I even met her. And Emma went on to describe how she came to know Alice through Facebook and through sisters of friends of sisters of friends.

Grandpa listened as Emma became more and more animated with her "offense," sharing everything she knew about Alice and how she had come to learn it. He realized that she was talking about things he never fully understood on earth. Of course, he knew about Facebook ... even knew two or three people who had joined it so they could see pictures of their grandchildren. But he certainly didn't make "friends" through Facebook. He made friends at church and at social night at the assisted living facility where Grandma still lived and by being neighbors and chatting with folks at the mailbox over the years.

It generally took him months to go from meeting someone to calling them an acquaintance, and it could be years later that he finally considered them friends. Even when friends gained that status, he'd be damned if he would have known that someone got dumped at a dance, or that they loved cats but were afraid of dogs, or that they dreamed of going to Rome someday. In his entire life, he had maybe at most considered 30-40 people friends, and most of those were during specific phases – grammar school, high school, college, then the times that his friends were the parents of his patients, and finally, those lazy relationships with people with whom he had grown old. There were very few whom he counted as lifelong friends. Emma, he knew, considered hundreds of people to be friends. Hadn't she proudly showed him a few months before he died when her Facebook friend count had hit 700?

He realized all of a sudden that she had stopped talking and seemed to be waiting for some kind of response from him. *Emma, my dear,* he said and his tone definitely softened. *A rule is a rule and, even if it doesn't make sense to you, think of the chaos there'd be if everyone just broke a rule because they thought it didn't or shouldn't apply to them.*

Emma thought for a minute. Finally she turned to him, and he saw that there were tears in her eyes. *But Grandpa,* she said and she sounded like the child she was. *I never asked to be here. It makes no sense to me that people my age, and even younger, die in the first place. At first, I was so confused ... and, honestly, I still don't understand how in the world any of this is fair. But I've accepted it. I know I'm here now, and here is where I have to stay. It seems like that's the BIG "have-to." I don't understand why there would be so many other have-to's. Especially have-to's that don't hurt other people ... in fact that make other people happy. Alice is happy to be friends with me. Honestly, Grandpa, in all the time I sat with Donovan and Joey at the school, I never once saw her smile. But when she hugged me, Grandpa, she was smiling and laughing, and I felt so happy. Surely there can't be anything too wrong with that? Maybe some of this stuff makes sense for all of you old people ...* Emma stopped abruptly and blushed, thinking maybe she had hurt Grandpa's feelings.

Go on, he said and patted her hand. *Don't you think I know that I'm old?* he asked with a chuckle.

Emma smiled back. *It's just that, well, the thing is ... you said I couldn't have experiences that I didn't have on earth? Well, on earth, I made friends. Lots of them. I worked really hard to be a good friend to my friends, and that wasn't always so easy. But it's who I was. I wasn't ever really great at anything ... not soccer, not basketball, not school, really. But I was a great friend. I didn't abandon my friends when I made new ones. I rarely questioned what they wanted ... I tried to want it, too. And when all those friends think about me now, what they wish for me the most is that I'm still having fun. And the thing is, Grandpa,* and Emma sighed with a weight no 19-year-old should have to bear, *the thing is, I'm pretty sure I can't have fun if I don't have friends.*

Oh, child, Grandpa sighed. *I understand. I do. But I don't make the rules.*

Then who does? asked Emma gently.

Well ... Grandpa started, then paused for a really long time ... Could it be? Was it possible? He was a learned man and considered himself one that didn't accept things on faith alone. *The truth is,* and Grandpa shook his head a little. *The truth is, I'm not sure. It's just the way it's always been.* And, as soon as he said those words out loud, he realized how hollow they sounded even to himself.

All right, he sighed after a few minutes of considering. *Let's handle it this way. I've only been here a little while myself. There are others who have been here way longer, and they are wiser and more experienced than I am. So keep your friend Alice for the moment, and I'll see what I can find out. I'll ask around and read up on it a little and see if I can find out why it's the way it is.* But, Emma, please, and with this, he took both her hands in his and stared her right in the eye. *Please be careful. Don't keep stirring the pot. Give me a little time. For now, only Alice, okay?*

Emma fidgeted. *Well, the thing is, Grandpa, I kind of made a few other friends. Now don't get mad ... Once Alice and I started to laugh and talk, the whole place kind of perked up and pretty soon everyone was kind of talking to everyone, and the thing is,* and she paused and took a deep breath. *The thing is, I'm kind of having a little get-together at my house tonight ... nothing big. Maybe 8 or 9 kids that's all* (and Emma held her breath hoping that Grandpa wasn't aware that, in Emma-speak, 8 or 9 almost always turned into 40 or 50 because friends had friends who had friends ...)

Grandpa closed his eyes and considered again. He had stopped watching after Emma's breakthrough with Alice because he was focused on how to handle that. *What now?* Finally, gruffly trying to maintain some sense of control, he asked, *Will Aunt Pat be there?*

Of course, Emma said sweetly, thinking to herself that Aunt Pat would probably join right in the fun.

Okay, but you have to be careful. Do you need me to go over the guidelines once more? It's possible, just possible, that maybe this one thing is okay given that you were such a professional friend and all, he smiled. *But don't go trying to push things too hard. Maybe the friend thing makes some kind of sense. But don't start doing anything more crazy. Remember – a good rule of thumb is to ask yourself, "Have I experienced this on earth?" If the answer is "no," be cautious. I'm telling you as sure as I'm sitting here, these are the kind of things that are going to get you in trouble.*

As Emma nodded, he kissed her on the forehead. *I love you,* he said gently, *and I want you to be happy. But I also want you to be safe, and there may be some things I just won't be able to protect you from. Be safe, sweet girl. Don't push. Enjoy your friends for the moment, and I'll be in touch.*

With that, he touched her cheek, kissed her gently again, and turned to go. *Lord, what a character,* he said to himself again and, in a blink of an eye, he was gone.

Emma

Emma drove home feeling pretty proud of herself. She had been uncertain about the consequences of the whole friend thing and expected to have to reckon with Grandpa Mebane about it at some point. She initially freaked out that it was right away but, in retrospect, she was kind of glad it happened as it did. She didn't have time to think about it too hard or even to make up some elaborate story about what happened. She hoped that she would have eventually landed on honesty being the best policy, but it happened so quickly that, really, honesty turned out to be the only choice. She was grateful that it seemed to have worked out, at least for the moment.

She probably should have felt more nervous, she realized. She still wondered if this whole place was run by God or some other force that might not take too kindly to her "breaking" the precious rules. But, really, she felt like if Grandpa was okay ... and it really seemed like he was ... then that was what mattered the most. He was in her corner, she knew, and mostly she felt good that she made him understand. He was smart. He would take it from here.

For the life of her she couldn't come up with what kind of cosmic reaction could be set off by the simple act of meeting people. She pondered it during the whole five-minute ride home from the high school but, by the time she pulled into the driveway, she figured she should just leave it to Grandpa to sort out. In the meantime, she had a party to get ready for!

A party ... how she missed dancing and singing and playing card games and sneaking in Icehouse beer through the basement windows. She wondered if Patsy would let them drink ... And what would happen if she got caught doing something that was against both the BEFORE <u>and</u> AFTER rules? She wondered if there were police here. She giggled kind of nervously. Whatever, this was going to be an interesting evening!

She shouted for Patsy as she set her keys down on the kitchen table. *We're in here, dear,* Patsy called back from the dining room.

We're?? Emma thought to herself. *Now what?* Surely Grandpa Mebane wasn't back again so soon. Maybe he changed his mind and recruited Patsy to help him try to stop the party from happening.

She peeked around the corner. There – unbelievable – just as adorable as they were on earth, sat Nanna and Grandaddy – her mom's grandparents who had been ancient the whole time Emma knew them. They were always perky though, she remembered, and she always believed that there was a core of young-at-heartedness beneath their wrinkly skin.

Oh my gosh ... Heeeeyyyyy, she said, and gave them each a quick kiss on the cheek. *What are you guys doing here?*

We came for the party, Nanna replied. *I'm going to make the snacks. I'm going to make celery with cheese whiz and*

*stuffed dates, and I even tucked away a little really good
artichoke spread just for a special occasion like this.*

OMG, *gross,* Emma thought to herself and tried to hide
her mild horror over not only the menu, but also her
realization that having Nanna and Grandaddy at her
party might just in fact be her "cosmic" punishment.
What irony, she thought, that her great-grandparents
arrived just as she was about to have her first real fun.

Grandaddy meanwhile had his ever-present tool kit.
I'm going to fix up the basement for you, he said with his
trademark twinkle in his eye. *This is going to be the best
damn party ever.*

Emma was more than a little conflicted. She loved
Nanna and Grandaddy, partly because her mom loved
them so. Her mom's mom married and divorced really
young, and they had both lived with Nanna and
Grandaddy for a long time after the divorce. Then, years
later, when her mom had Jason as a single parent, she
lived with Nanna and Grandaddy again because her own
parents were in Japan.

Emma's personal experience of Nanna was a little
mixed – she was nice enough and kind of funny, but
everything had to be so ridiculously neat at her house,
and talk about rules! Nanna and Grandaddy had a house
for years at the Jersey shore, and her mom told her about
how Nanna would only let them go to the beach between
11:00 and 2:00 and never when the west wind was
blowing, and you could never, ever have more than one
egg for breakfast, and the TV could only be on for a half
hour a day, and on and on.

Grandaddy, on the other hand, was every kid's dream. He was always whistling and smiling, and there was that twinkle in his eye that made it seem like everything was one big joke and that you and he were the only ones in the know. He snuck you your favorite candy the same way he used to sneak cigarettes behind the garage – everyone knew about it, even Nanna, but everyone, even Nanna, just kind of looked the other way 'cause, like many others, Nanna was totally charmed by Grandaddy – from the time he proposed back in the 1930s, through 75 years of marriage, to her death in 2002 (complications from a broken hip). Within six months, Grandaddy had joined Nanna in AFTER.

Now, they looked just like she remembered from the last time she saw them. Grandaddy had his arm around Nanna's shoulder, and she kept reaching up and patting his hand.

Okay ... Emma decided she was genuinely happy to see them, but this was definitely a dilemma.

Look, she said, *I am super excited about all the treats. But really you can't be here for this party. It's my first one ever in* AFTER *and, honestly, how popular do you think you would have been if your great-grandparents came to your parties?* She looked right at Grandaddy when she said it with her best from-one-party-lover-to-another-you-gotta-help-me-out face.

And, bless him, he jumped right in on her side. *Betty, Patsy, Emma is 100 percent right about this. So here's what we're going to do. We need to help Emma get ready, and then we need to stay out of her hair.* With a wink at Emma, he said, *Don't worry, sweetie. We'll make ourselves good and scarce!*

Once that was agreed, Emma got pretty excited about them all helping her get ready. She talked Nanna out of the menu she had originally proposed and into all of Emma's favorites – nutballs and shortbread and mini-Reubens. She and Grandaddy headed to the basement. They pushed the pool table against the wall, and Grandaddy whipped up an awesome dance floor and even put up an old fashioned disco ball that he figured out how to synch up with her iPod. The result was, well, otherworldly.

Patsy helped Emma pick out a super flattering outfit and, as the evening approached, Emma's heart was full of love for her "new" family and full of excitement about seeing her new friends. In fact, she was feeling so magnanimous that she asked Patsy to run to the church and pick up Sammy, figuring worst case he could be the runner between the kitchen and the basement, bringing Nanna's concoctions down and the empty plates back up.

As the time for the party approached, Emma began to get more and more jittery. What if she had misread the situation? What if Alice was just being nice and had no intention of coming over? What if someone had stepped in and talked them out of coming and everything would go back to the way it was and she'd have to start all over again? What if ...

Emma was interrupted from the early stages of panic by the doorbell ringing simultaneously with Duck running to his doggie toy box to stuff his mouth with gifts for the guests. Emma sent her family upstairs to the bedrooms, ran to the door, gave herself a final glance in the hall mirror, and assumed as casual a stance as she could.

Alice! Bobbie! Oh, hi, Sandy. Hey, Andy, Jack ... Hi, Flynn, she said, almost shyly, but he just kind of slipped past her with just a quick nod. *It's this way,* she said gaily, and they all followed her down into the basement. As she had BEFORE, she left a sign on the front door – saying *Welcome, Come On In, We're Downstairs* – and, just as was the case back then, she had to get some help from the adults after about 10 minutes to start turning people away. Even her newly souped-up basement couldn't hold every dead teenager in the State of Illinois and, really, some of the steady stream of party seekers looked a little shady.

If they don't know my name, don't let them in, Emma instructed and, in truth, most of the "strangers" didn't know her name but simply asked if this was where the "girl who makes friends" lived. That was a dead giveaway to Grandaddy that they should not be allowed in and, after a few minutes, the line outside the door was so long that Grandaddy shooed them all away, turned off the lights, and locked the door. *Good grief,* he thought, and for him there were no mixed feelings. *What a gal!*

In the meantime, the basement was rocking! Apparently no one had danced since they'd left their BEFOREs, and the pent up energy was almost electrical. No one had time to drink beer, which was A-OK by Emma, as she hadn't quite worked out what might happen if they did and got caught. They all just sang and danced and hugged and sang some more.

Periodically, Emma would try to dance her way over
to get closer to Flynn, but he seemed to be mostly paying
attention to Sammy, making sure he was having fun.
They tossed darts and leafed through some of Ben's DVDs
and, at one point, it looked like Flynn was trying to teach
him how to dance. Emma couldn't believe it. Flynn was
totally the hottest guy in the room – tall, kind of skinny,
with piercing blue eyes and dark, curly hair that was
clearly reddish when the light caught it a certain way –
and here he was being a total sweetie pie with Sammy.
She was definitely a sucker for gingers and totally a
sucker for nice guys, and he was clearly both. The fact
that he was systematically ignoring her didn't hurt either,
as she was a girl who loved a challenge. Eventually she
would find out more about him from Alice, but, for now,
she wasn't going to obsess about it.

She lost herself in the music again. At one point, they
all started to do some kind of line dance to *Billie Jean* –
amazing how everyone just seemed to know it – and
Jack, Emma, and Alice started to regale everyone with
their moon walks. Emma started giggling so hard she lost
her balance and fell back a little into the corner and
realized with a jolt that she had backed into Michael
Jackson. It wasn't a download of *Billy Jean* that was
playing in the background. It was Michael Jackson
actually singing. THE Michael Jackson. Michael Jackson
was singing *Billy Jean* at her party in her basement in the
middle of Geneva, Illinois! *Wow,* she thought giddily. *We
are so not in Kansas anymore!*

At just about the same time that she realized Michael
Jackson was in her basement, everyone else did, too, and

suddenly pandemonium broke out. Everyone was clamoring to get to Michael and touch him or get his autograph or get a picture next to him. At one point, one of the guys she didn't know, and who somehow managed to slip in past Grandaddy, yelled that he could top this and, before you knew it, Elvis was singing in the other corner, and then someone really went over the top and Kurt Cobain was playing guitar on top of the bar.

Within minutes, everything got completely out of control, and people were actually kind of trampling on each other to get into position around one of the dead singers who all just kept singing louder and louder. It was getting kind of scary. Out of the corner of her eye, Emma noticed that Flynn pulled Sammy out of the way onto the landing at the top of the stairs, so at least she knew he was safe. And, just as she was about to completely freak out, the lights went on, and Grandaddy was there!

You all need to leave, right now! Grandaddy said sternly, and he had his hammer in one hand and was kind of tapping it onto the palm of the other. Truth be known, he looked a little silly, but the very presence of an adult brought an immediate semblance of order. Everyone started to calm down. Once Nanna arrived to reinforce Grandaddy (Aunt Pat was too busy trying to get autographs to be much help), the kids all started to collect their stuff, and even the singers looked a little sheepish as they all filed out past the grown-up patrol and up the stairs. Alice and Flynn and Sammy hung back a little, and Grandaddy said that they could stay and help clean up.

Even with the abrupt ending, Emma and Alice agreed that it had been a great party, and Flynn seemed to soften his attitude toward Emma a little as he uprighted over-turned chairs and swept Reuben remnants up off the floor. When they were through, he agreed to take Sammy and Alice home. Alice promised to call the next day, and Emma was happier than she had been since the night when she giggled for hours with Sarah and Ben before that morning when everything changed.

Her warm feelings from that night – the last night she was sure that Ben had laughed – started to merge with her happiness from this night. Perhaps because she had spent so much time in the "Ben-and-Emma" basement, she suddenly felt a strong, distinct, and overwhelmingly positive connection to Ben begin to take shape. She thought of Ben's room. Just as she had during her parties before she died, she told everyone tonight that his bedroom (a separate room in the basement) was strictly off limits.

She herself hadn't gone near it since BEFORE. She hadn't felt that she could handle it. But, tonight, for some reason, she felt drawn to it. Suddenly, she knew that Ben's room would be a place of comfort, a place that would in some way bring her peace and strength.

As she allowed her mind to shut off the thoughts that had been swirling almost nonstop, and as she allowed her heart to release a layer of its ever-present heaviness, she tiptoed back to the basement, stood for a few minutes to gather courage outside the closed door to Ben's room and, with a nod of resolve, pulled it open and then disappeared inside.

Ben / Emma

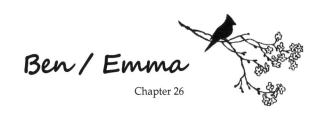

Chapter 26

Ben's room was very dark, but Emma immediately realized that he was there with her. She heard Duck thump his tail and, as her eyes adjusted to the dark, she realized that Ben was asleep in his bed with Duck by his side.

She sat down next to him on the bed, feeling strong and confident. She instinctively knew that she was about to experience Ben in the same way that she had her dad in the hospital that day and she was ready. Perhaps because she had merged happiness from BEFORE with her first pure happiness in AFTER, she knew that, this time, she was strong enough to reach him the right way. Or perhaps Duck had been the missing part that would enable her to finally break through. Or perhaps it was because it had been a very good day and her heart was overflowing with happiness to be with Ben. For whatever the reason, she knew that she was on the cusp of something truly important to him ... and to her.

She reached out and touched his forehead. He was so sad. His sleep was fitful, and his sighs were heart-wrenching. She let herself be pulled into his grief, to experience his anguish as her own, just as she had with her dad. The difference was that, in the hospital, she had been afraid and uncertain and every bit as sad as her dad.

Tonight, she was strong, and she hoped that somehow her strength could help her brother. She wanted to wrap her love around his fragile heart and give back to him even a small piece of all that he had given to her. As with her dad, she experienced Ben in a profound way that was beyond human connection. She understood his guilt, his regret, even his sadness.

His guilt seemed to stem from little things he hadn't done ... convinced her to go into the hot tub that night, downloaded the movies she had wanted for her trip, traded for her counter shift so she could sleep in a little since she was so tired ...

His regret was more complicated. He believed that they had only recently come to like each other so much. Oh, they always loved each other. But love combined with like was way more powerful than either one alone. He regretted that he hadn't let her know how much he <u>liked</u> her ... that he really had come to find her funny and smart and trustworthy. He regretted that she may not have known how much he enjoyed her company and appreciated her advice, her taste in music, and the shows she had turned him on to.

She also understood that he saw her death as symbolic of the end of his own childhood, and he regretted that he let it slip away without them doing enough goofy things together. She had always wanted to play, but he rarely let himself join in. What had he given up for following rules and being the "responsible" one and not letting his guard down? What would he become without the part of himself that she knew how to tease out of him? Now that she was gone, and he was suddenly a grown-up, would he now never have fun again? Had he learned enough about frivolity and laughter and lightness that he would someday be able to "do" happy on his own?

His sadness was the most complex feeling he was having, and she needed to get a little closer to him to understand it. She lay down next to him and wrapped her arms around him, pulling Duck a little closer so that they were all three touching. She immediately experienced feelings she understood intimately because they reflected her own. They had been so happy. Her brother, her sister, her mom, and her dad. It was just plain sad that she had been ripped away from a family who loved each other so much. It was just plain sad that things would never again be like they were ... not for Ben, not for her, not for anyone whom she had loved and who had loved her back.

He was sad for all that he had lost, but also for his mom, his dad, and Sarah. And he was so, so sad for her. He kept replaying all of the things she would never do ... she would never graduate from college, she would never be a true artist, she would never go to Outback or hear the new fun. song, *We Are Young*, which she would have loved so much. He kept thinking that she would never marry, that she would never have a wedding, or a baby of her own, or even the new car she told him to start working on her parents to buy her for college graduation. She would never, ever know true romantic love ...

... and here it got even more complicated. Emma realized that Ben's sadness that she would never know love was mixed up with his own sadness that he, too, would never know love. He needed to stay sad, he needed to stay lonely, he needed to keep turning away ... turning away from Alex ... because there was no room to fit in love when his heart was so full of the loss of Emma.

Emma was so stunned that she accidentally pulled away before she could find a way to make Ben feel better. Ben was always such a logical thinker. He was always so smart. How in the world had he gotten so mixed up? Emma didn't know a lot about romantic love, but this she knew – it could fit in with just about any other feeling! For Ben to think that somehow he couldn't let himself love Alex because Emma was gone was just plain crazy.

Hmmm, it was going to be a little tougher than she thought to help Ben. Apparently, it was going to take more than just figuring out a way to let him know that she was okay. Apparently, he had mixed up his grief with his feelings for Alex.

Emma thought and thought. She had never considered herself to be a great idea person, and a part of her acknowledged that most of her plans didn't really work the way they should. But hadn't she figured out how to stay connected with Sarah? And what about Alice? They were now friends and, even better, Alice was clearly friends with Flynn and Emma definitely had high hopes for Flynn.

Wait ...

Clearly a big part of Ben's grief was about things that could now never happen for her, and one of those BIG things, from which many of the others could come (a wedding, a husband, a baby, her own home), was finding true love. What if she could make that happen? She knew that there were serious hurdles to overcome and it could take a while and maybe Flynn wasn't even "the one." (She didn't even let herself think just now about another Grandpa Mebane moment.)

But what if she could speed things up, if she could somehow push the whole Ben and Alex thing? She knew they were so close to being in love. She had been pretty sure that Alex had fallen for Ben, and she now knew for a fact that Ben loved Alex. What if she could help them take that final step that deep down both of them really wanted to take? And what if somehow their being in love helped her break down the whole you-can't-experience-it-because-you-didn't-know-it-on-earth thing?

For her, Ben epitomized the qualities she wanted in a boyfriend, and she had spent many hours wishing that she could find someone just like him. *(Okay, who also liked beer and people, but still ...)* The more she thought about it, the more she became convinced that somehow this could all be connected. She could almost visualize a double wedding – her walking down the aisle with Flynn in AFTER at the same time that Ben was marrying Alex in BEFORE. *What a total trip that would be!*

She realized that the whole thing might be a tiny bit convoluted, but it seemed a lot less crazy than Ben trying to keep Alex away because somehow it made sense that it would be better for Emma. Now that was nuts. And although her plan might not be perfect, she was filled with the same hope and resolve she had when she had decided she was going to get Sarah back. This really was turning into one big adventure. But now it was an adventure with purpose!

She gave Ben a hug. *I'll be back,* she whispered. *I love you.* She whistled softly to Duck. *Come on, boy. We've got some planning to do!*

Alice

Chapter 27

Tears were streaming down Alice's face because she was laughing so hard at Emma's recap of the antics she had tried over the last few weeks to get Ben and Alex together. The girls were lounging around in the hot tub enjoying another picture-perfect day. Emma and Alice saw each other almost every day, but this was the first time Emma opened up about her plan to link Ben and Alex, Flynn and her. All of her attempts had failed so far, but they made funny stories, and this one was hilarious.

You should have seen Doug's face, Emma said giggling. *He had no idea what was going on. Every time a song came on, it was a love song and not just any love song. Love songs that were totally over the top so Ben and Alex would be sure to get the message. I sent "I Will Always Love You" and "When a Man Loves a Woman" and "Unchained Melody" – perfect. I loved "Unchained Melody" so much I sent it twice in a row, and that's when Doug kind of freaked out. I heard him mutter, "What the hell's going on? Where'd all these sappy love songs come from?" He kept going back to the sound system and try- ing to skip ahead on the CD, but I just kept them coming. I never heard him cuss so much! Finally, he pulled the plug out. I almost sent another one, but I thought he might have a heart attack, so I gave up on that plan.*

I love "Unchained Melody," Alice said, and the girls took a pause in Emma's recap so they could sing a little duet.

They were laughing so hard, Emma got the hiccups, so she got out of the hot tub to go get some cold water.

While she was gone, Alice reflected on how quickly they had grown close over the last few weeks, since Emma's now famous party.

~

Until Emma, Alice had been really depressed. She had missed her old friends so much that she hurt most of the time. Not like the cancer that had eventually killed her. When she got to AFTER, all of her physical pain had disappeared. But there was still a hole in her heart where her friends had been. They had been so loyal, even as she deteriorated more and more. Finally, when she didn't even have the strength to talk, they came to read to her or to hold her hand or to just sit quietly and watch her sleep. She had hung in for seven months past when she should have died, and she knew in her heart it was their love that kept her alive.

But she hadn't had the energy to have real fun with her friends in a long time. And it was possible, she reflected, that even before she got sick they hadn't had the kind of fun she had with Emma. Emma was easy to be with. She was funny and kind, and she just seemed so content to be with Alice. Emma made her feel like she was the best friend Emma ever had, even though Alice knew that Emma had lots of best friends. They all still posted on her Facebook Wall, and Emma often filled Alice in on the details behind the good times that her friends described. Emma's crowd seemed a little faster than Alice's, but there was no doubt that they embraced life wholeheartedly.

~

Despite the beautiful day, the relaxing warmth of the hot tub, and the giggles she and Emma had shared all day long, Alice was feeling a little uneasy. She just didn't think Emma's plan for matchmaking was all that sound, and she knew that Emma was really counting on it to work. If you could make something happen by sheer willpower, it possibly had a chance, but there were so many holes in it.

It was possible, she supposed, that Emma could nudge Ben and Alex together. It sounded like they were already headed for love, and Emma might be able to speed things up. Emma might even be the one to get around the widely known rule that you couldn't experience new things in AFTER. She had, after all, already bent the rule to fit her "interpretation" when she broke through with Alice and, so far, there hadn't been any consequences. No, if anyone could do it, it would be Emma. The real problem, she knew, was going to be Flynn.

There was simply no way that Flynn would fall for Emma. There was so much going on in his head – he had too much guilt, for one thing. He died in a car accident, and he was driving. He and his girlfriend had been partying and, despite her arguing, he insisted on driving them home. He lost control, and his car slammed into a tree. He died instantly. His girlfriend, Debbie, had lived. However, she was left physically paralyzed, and Flynn became emotionally so.

Alice hadn't known Flynn very well BEFORE, although they went to the same high school. He was the proverbial "catch," and he hung out with the most popular kids. He never struck her as particularly kind or thoughtful, but she was the only one his age he knew in AFTER and, as she got to know him more, she realized that he had a wistfulness about him that was endearing, though it served to keep her at arms length. Perhaps Emma could reach him, but Alice sincerely doubted it. Not while Debbie was alive and suffering.

Just then Emma came back and got back in the hot tub. *So, let me tell you this last idea,* she started, as though she had never been gone. (Apparently the cold water was successful because her hiccups had disappeared.) *I'm pretty sure this is brilliant!* Emma proceeded to tell Alice that she finally "called" Grandaddy (whom Alice had met the night of the party) ...

~

Nanna and Grandaddy had gone home after the party but, before he left, Grandaddy gave Emma a huge conch shell from their beach house and told her that, if she ever needed him, all she had to do was blow it and he would arrive instantly. Emma asked if wouldn't it be better to just call, but Grandaddy said, no, he didn't have a cell phone, and they had never had a regular phone at the shore.

Emma had resisted calling Grandaddy, partly because the conch shell was so corny. But, finally, she ran out of ideas, and she knew asking Grandpa Mebane was totally not an option. So, reluctantly, she put the shell up to her lips and blew ... and Grandaddy appeared instantly.

I know just the thing, Grandaddy said immediately after Emma described what she was trying to do. *It's kind of a two-step process. But we can get started right now.*

First, he and Emma drove to Alex's house where he told Emma to do something to Alex's computer to temporarily put it on the blink. *If it were up to me,* he said, *I'd mess with her plumbing a bit, but I don't think Ben could help with that, and this idea hinges on Alex turning to Ben for help.*

Emma thought for a bit and came up with just the thing. She knew that Ben had helped Alex set up an external hard drive she had purchased a few months ago and on which she stored all of her pictures, music, and movies. Emma played around for a few minutes with Alex's computer until it was no longer able to recognize the hard drive. Emma knew that Ben would be able to fix Alex's because he had fixed a similar problem for Emma before she went away to college.

That should do it, Emma said. *Ben knows a lot about computers, and Alex will know right away that she has a problem so it won't take long before she asks him to help.*

Perfect, said Grandaddy. *Now we just have to speed things up a little. When do Ben and Alex work together again?*

Tomorrow, answered Emma.

Okay, cookie. Do a quick check in tonight to make sure that Alex discovers our handiwork. Then call me, and I'll be back. This is going to work. We make quite a team!

Alex tried unsuccessfully to watch a movie on her computer that very night, so the next day Emma blew on the shell again *(OMG),* and she and Grandaddy headed to Town House. Grandaddy fooled around with Alex's car a little, pulling out a wire here and there.

That should do it, he winked at Emma. *Anyone who knows anything about a car will be able to fix this right away.*

But in the meantime, she'll freak out a little, and Ben will gallantly take her home. Hopefully, when they get to her house, she'll mention the hard drive. I think you should be waiting for them. I'm not exactly sure what should happen next, but you'll be able to think of something. You'll have them alone in her house and with Alex all grateful and happy and Ben feeling all manly and competent.

~

... And that's just what happened, Emma told Alice. *They walked out together, and Ben (he's such a gentleman!) waited until she started her car, which of course wouldn't start. So, he took her home, and she did ask him in for some lemonade and of course mentioned in passing that the hard drive was acting weird, and Ben said he thought he could fix it and started working on it right away.*

While Ben was working, I tried to push Alex into Ben, but I just didn't have the strength to make that happen. I'm not sure I could even touch her – my hand just kind of went through her. Finally, she sat down next to Ben and her hand was resting right next to his on the table. I kept trying to pull Ben's hand closer to her hand, but it just wasn't happening. I was getting pretty frustrated when I realized that all that pulling at Ben's arm – and missing – had kind of loosened the leather bracelet I had brought him from London. I couldn't do much with it, but I could do way more than trying to touch him directly, so there must be something about things I actually gave people. (I made a mental note that when I had more time I should work on messing with things like that to see if that might be a new way to communicate.)

Anyhow, I must have loosened it more than I thought because, when he was cleaning up, it fell off. He didn't notice it. But he will. I have a good feeling about this. He'll eventually go back, of course, and who knows what will happen then? ... What do you think?

Alice was impressed with the elaborateness of the plan though she secretly thought it left a little too much to chance. But Emma was happy so she was happy, and she prayed with all her heart that it would work out. Emma deserved some good luck.

As they got out of the hot tub and were drying off, Alice said, *Let's go get a little ice cream for luck,* and gave Emma a spontaneous hug.

What's that for? Emma asked with a smile as she hugged her back

It's just for being my friend, Alice answered. *It's just because I'm so glad you came into my life.*

Emma grinned, and Alice (not for the first time) thanked her lucky stars that Emma had found a way to find her.

Rod

Chapter 28

Rod was lost in reflection as he prepared the grill for the weekly Sunday cookout. Sarah was home again for a visit, and things felt more complete than they did when she was gone. Much as he loved Ben, Rod struggled when family was defined as just Ben and him. Donna was still in London and, in a weird sort of way, her absence made Emma's absence feel a little less ... permanent somehow. At some level, even though he knew it was ridiculous, Rod held out some kind of weird hope that, once Donna came back and took her place at the dinner table, somehow Emma would be there, too, filling the empty seat that loomed so large.

It's not that he and Ben hadn't fallen into some kind of rhythm. They would chat for a few minutes before Ben went to work in the morning, and Rod attempted to make dinner for Ben once or twice a week. More often than not, however, they'd get fast food on their own and retreat to separate rooms. Ben would emerge toward bedtime to offer to pick up something for dessert or to ask how the Cubs did but, for the most part, he kept to himself.

Recently, Ben and he had started eating dinner while watching TV together, which felt like a step forward. Ben seemed to be making more of an effort to connect and, every once in a while, he seemed like his old self. Rod still worried about the deep circles under his eyes, and he longed to hear Ben's old laugh. It's not that they never laughed. They did. But it was often almost uncomfortable, and neither laughed for long – likely, Rod knew, because it seemed disrespectful to Emma.

Again, a crazy thought. Emma would want them to laugh. Emma would want them to be as they were. But, despite wishing he could be everything that Emma would want, he knew that would never be. They might learn to function again – in fact, they had all taken baby steps in that direction. But, although broken hearts could heal, they would have to do so by forming plenty of scar tissue. That, he knew, was going to take a long, long time.

He did what he could to hold the family together and to keep Emma's memory front and center. But it wasn't easy, and he often felt that he was the only one who got it. Didn't they pick out the poem, *Death is Nothing at All*, to read at Emma's funeral? Didn't it say that we should speak her name in the "easy way that we always did"? Didn't Donna herself select the reading because she wanted to be sure that we "laugh as we always laughed at the little jokes we enjoyed together"? He remembered her squeezing his hand a little when the minister read the last few lines:

Life means all that it ever meant. It is the same as it ever was – there is unbroken continuity. Why should I be out of mind because I am out of sight? I am waiting for you, for an interval, somewhere very near, just round the corner. All is well.

Why weren't they working harder to make that sentiment live? It's not that Emma was out of anyone's mind.

But, really, for them, "all" was decidedly about as far as you could get from "well." And they definitely seemed stuck where they were.

He didn't expect it to be easy, and he certainly couldn't help visiting his own dark places on a daily basis. But it sometimes seemed that he was the only one who was making an effort to find a positive place for Emma in a new way in their new definition of family. And it was exhausting.

He was glad that Donna went back to London. He had encouraged her primarily because he truly believed that it was the best thing for her. She wasn't ready to face a home or even a Geneva that didn't have Emma in it. But a part of him knew it also would help him for her to be gone. She was so depressed – she stayed in bed for days and seemed to feel like she had accomplished something if she took a shower or changed her clothes. He was pleased that, over time, she was able to focus her energy well enough to get through each day at work, but there was nothing left when she got home. Her missing Emma was heart-wrenching and almost feral. He was powerless to ease the depth of her pain and was a little frightened by it.

He now understood emotionally what he had previously only understood intellectually – people grieve in very different ways. Each person's journey is a personal one, no matter how close they are to others who love them and who want to help. He hoped that the passing of time would enable Donna to forge a path through her grief that could coexist with his own and that they could find a way to help each other as they had at so many other points during the course of their 32-year marriage.

He also hoped that his family was strong enough to hold together during this time when they simultaneously needed each other more than they ever had and yet were the least equipped to help one other because they were so focused on helping themselves.

For now, he was left to shape his own journey and to keep finding ways to show Jason and Sarah and Ben how much he loved them, how much they mattered. And, of course, he worked tirelessly to honor Emma.

His preferred way to handle a challenge was to keep busy – he found that it was when he was idle that he was most debilitated. It pleased him to align his activity with anything to do with Emma, and it brought him comfort to be connected with her in a way that led to a concrete outcome. So, for example, he created a garden around the red bud tree that Donna's parents had arranged to be planted in the back yard, and he tended to the "Emma Tree" religiously. Also, he was sorting through everything "Emma" he could lay his hands on – her computer, her photos, her text messages, even her games and her HeyTells. He was delighted he had kept every piece of her art work from the time she was a toddler through to the true beauties she had created in high school. He sorted and resorted all the portfolios that held these treasures.

He made a commitment to himself that he would use Emma's art to help her achieve her dream to be recognized as an artist. He started by publishing *A Book Abot Chaps* – a little gem that Emma herself had discovered within the last couple of years in Donna's nightstand. She had laughed and laughed and passed the little book around to all her friends, who all wanted their own copy. Fortunately, he had wrested it back, and he set it up on a table at her viewing during which it became a source of warmly remembered joy. Once again, the little book that got just about everything wrong seemed very right. After he published it, he sent copies to all of Emma's friends, and the original occupied an honored spot in the corner for Emma he had set up in the family room.

As he brought in the burgers that he had apparently cooked by rote, he called Ben and Sarah for dinner, and he paused to look over at Emma's corner ... and what was left of Emma in the box that held her ashes. As usual, his feelings were mixed, but he quickly got a grip on his pain. He thought it was important that they looked grief right in the eye on a regular basis and practice not blinking. He also wanted a spot that her friends could visit – they had not yet decided whether to have a grave site or another place where people to go to "be" with Emma. So, for now, they came here to 1616 Forest Lane where Emma had lived and laughed and loved. It seemed right somehow.

It was also the spot where he hoped his family could find comfort some day. It held her watch and her rings and her bracelets. It held her gift cards that reminded everyone of all of her favorite places. It held little mementos of important times in her life – concert ticket stubs, pictures of her trip to Ireland, the little things she had already bought for her first apartment. It held dried flowers from her casket and special little gifts she had given to Donna and to him last Christmas. And it held things that Emma's friends brought to honor her on visits to sit and to remember. He wouldn't say that it had totally caught on with Ben and Sarah yet ... but he had faith that it would.

They sat at the kitchen table to eat dinner, and he was pleased that Ben and Sarah slipped into some light bantering about whether book three of *The Hunger Games* was the best of the series (Ben) or disappointingly tidy (Sarah). Really, it wouldn't be all that hard to pretend Emma had just gone back to school pissed because she had to leave before the cookout was ready. Rod sighed and recognized that there was a little bit of hope in that sigh.

Once Sarah and Ben had finished their debate about *The Hunger Games*, they moved on to their current passion – *Game of Thrones*. They talked about *Game of Thrones* a lot, mostly because Sarah couldn't keep any of the characters straight and Ben could remember every detail about every weapon, every family, and every war. They had made a commitment to read the same number of chapters each night, but Sarah kept getting distracted and Ben, though he was honor bound not to read farther than agreed, kept wanting to up the daily reading allotment because he was so into it.

Okay, so who is Ser Brynden again? Sarah asked, and Ben replied, *You mean the Blackfish?* Sarah answered, *... Maybe,* and Ben said, *He's Lord Hoster Tully's younger brother.* And Sarah asked, *Oh, okay ... And who is that?* So, Ben explained, *Catelyn's father. They currently hold River-*

run. To which Sarah said, *Ohhh, okay, I gotcha. And how long has he been with Robb? Blackfins, I mean ...*

Ben started to laugh. *Have you read any of this book?* he asked. *It sure sounds like you're reading a different book than I am!*

This easy jostling went back and forth for a while, and Rod was lulled into a feeling that felt remarkably like being happy ... or at least not sad. *Let's go get some ice cream,* he suggested, and Sarah and Ben readily agreed. It was a beautiful night, and Rod realized that he was ridiculously excited about leaving the house for something other than work.

As Ben started to clear his plate from the table, Sarah casually asked, *Where's your bracelet?* Ben stopped in his tracks. He looked down at his wrist and paled visibly. *Oh my gosh,* he said. *I don't know,* and the weight of the world was in his words. Sarah touched his arm. *We'll find it,* she promised. *When did you last see it?*

Rod let go of his hopes for a family outing and began to organize the search.

Ben

Ben's heart was hammering in his chest. He had turned the house upside down looking for his bracelet, and it was nowhere to be found. *This is not happening,* he kept saying to himself. He had lost his sister. What kind of bad joke would it be that he would also lose the bracelet that was her last and best gift to him?

Could you have left it at work? Dad asked.

No, I know I had it at Alex's house because she commented on how much she liked it. I texted her, and she's looking for it, too. I'm gonna head over and help her look.

Do you want me to come help? asked Sarah.

No, I'll text you if I find it.

On the way to Alex's house, Ben actually said a little he supposed you could call it "prayer" to Emma. *Emma, please help me find this damn bracelet,* he said out loud. *Would that be so hard? I'm doing the best I can. I need that bracelet.*

When he got to Alex's house, he sat in the car for a minute gathering himself. He found that he didn't always think completely clearly when Alex was around. On top of that, if the bracelet wasn't there, he would know that he really had lost it, and he mentally prepared himself to try to hold it together if that was the case.

As he rang the doorbell, he said again, *Emma, please ...*

Alex opened the door, and there it was. She was holding it in her hand and grinning from ear to ear. *I found it,* she said simply and gave him a big hug. *I found your sister's bracelet.*

To his utter chagrin, Ben started to cry, and Alex hugged him even harder. *I know,* she said. *I know ...*

The emotions he had held so tightly in check came spilling out, and he started to say all the things he had kept so deeply held in his heart.

They talked for hours. Ben felt as though he had never had so much to say. He talked about what it was like to have a sister like Emma – the joys were easy to talk about, but he also opened up about the challenges. He talked about how hard it was to be a big brother to her because she was always on the cusp of getting into some kind of trouble even as a little girl when she would skip across the street without looking or forget to shut the freezer door on a hot summer day or throw her arms around a stranger's dog she happened onto at the park.

He had almost resented her when they were young. She was the one people were drawn to and he was the one they thought odd. True, she was a chatterbox and he rarely talked. (He shared with Alex that his kindergarten teacher had called his parents after a few weeks after school started to recommend speech therapy because she thought Ben *couldn't* talk, not realizing that he just chose not to talk since he didn't feel he had anything to say.) True, she could best be described as "sunny" and he perhaps as "cloudy." But, damn it! He played it safe. And she didn't. He had accepted from early childhood that his job was to protect her and keep her safe. And, after working so hard to do just that, after the years he had spent worrying about her, after the years they had spent forgiving each other their differences and then the years they had spent rejoicing in them ... after all that, he had failed her. Somehow, she had slipped away.

And, throughout all of his talk, his tears, and his silences, Alex was there. She didn't turn away. She didn't try to rationalize his feelings of guilt, and she didn't try to pretend that her words could help his grief. She didn't argue with his logic (which even he realized was a bit crazy at times), and she wasn't put off by the rawness of his emotions. At some point, he realized that she was holding his hand, and a little later he understood that it was right for her to be doing so.

Eventually, Ben simply ran out of steam. He was spent, and he was empty of every feeling he had kept bottled up inside. What was left was a kind of exhausted peace that he hadn't felt in a long time, maybe ever. He felt both more vulnerable and at the same time more safe than he ever had before. They sat for a while in silence. At one point, he became aware of the song playing in the background.

> *And one day we will die*
> *And our ashes will fly from the aeroplane over the sea*
> *But for now we are young*
> *Let us lay in the sun*
> *And count every beautiful thing we can see*
> *Love to be*
> *In the arms of all I'm keeping here with me*

It was the song that inspired the design for the tattoo on his arm – the arm that was now resting lightly around

Alex. He felt confused. He had picked the song to honor Emma but, now listening to it, he understood its complexity at a different level. She had been young, and she had laid in the sun. Had he ever done that? Was it his time? Would he honor Emma more if he let a little of her light shine through in him?

He didn't know. He was too tired to think. He could just feel. And what he felt was grateful ... Alex was there. She had seen him at his worst, and she had not looked away. Surely it was wrong not to look back ...

He pulled her close and closed his eyes and just let himself feel the essence of Alex. She raised her face to his and lightly touched his cheek. *I'm so tired,* he said. *I know,* she answered. She stood and pulled him up. *You should rest,* she said, and he nodded. She led him into her room and lay down next to him. *Close your eyes,* she whispered. *I'm here ...*

As he drifted off to sleep, he had one final image of Emma. She was young ... she was beautiful ... she was lying in the sun ... and she was smiling.

Emma

Chapter 30

Emma was alone in the house for the first time since BEFORE. She and Aunt Pat agreed to a short trial separation because Aunt Pat wanted to be back in her own home for a while. She was anxious to be closer to her great-grandbabies, and she wanted to experiment in her own space to try to connect with her kids and her sister in ways Emma had discovered.

Although Emma was equally anxious to have her own alone time, she and Aunt Pat both cried when they said goodbye, and even Honey hung her head a little. Patsy had become Emma's friend, her confidante, and her surrogate mom, and it would be challenging in many ways not to see her every day. For her part, Pat would miss Emma's sunny presence, her sense of adventure, and the laughter that seemed to surround everything she said and did. Fortunately, they had agreed that the separation would be short-term. In their heart of hearts, they both thought Patsy would be back soon, and likely to stay.

So, this morning, Aunt Pat had left the way she had come. One minute she was there, the next minute she was gone. Emma didn't really have time to give her a proper Mebane Send-off, though she did give her a quick hug.

That hug lingered in her mind and quite naturally caused her to reflect on the first time she had seen Aunt Pat. Could it really have been only three months ago?

Time was kind of funny in AFTER. Her only sense of its passage was through Facebook entries and key events when family and friends were together and missing her as much as she missed them.

She knew she had missed her father's birthday, the first day of her sophomore year, and Sarah's birthday. She participated as best she could, but these key times were definitely the most painful and she tried not to think much about them until they were upon her. The times in between had definitely gotten way better now that she had friends.

She felt she had grown more in these three months than in any time she could remember in her whole life. Her brain was definitely working overtime most of the time, and she was particularly proud of the things she had figured out on her own – how to send messages through music, how to use dream visits to stay connected with Sarah, and her crowning achievement ... how to make new friends.

There were definitely things that were still pretty much unresolved. Grandpa, for example, was still trying to sort out whether she would be in any kind of trouble over the whole friend thing but, as Emma thought of Alice and Jack and Sandy and (especially) Flynn, she knew that it had been worth it ... whatever the consequences.

She had been able to reach many of the people who loved her – Sarah, Dad, Jason, Kevin, Paige, Steffanie, Taylor, Mel, Alexa, and Carrie. They had breakthroughs of awareness that on some level she would always be with them. She just had to perfect it so that she could communicate more at will and stretch their moments of hope into longer periods of peace and understanding.

She felt that she had done what she could with Ben for now. She firmly believed that her nudge would work and that Ben and Alex would find their way to each other. What she didn't know was whether that would help her find love with Flynn. That was majorly unresolved!

Emma also knew that plenty of the people who loved her couldn't get past their pain yet, and thoughts of her were still so dark she couldn't seem to find a way to connect with them. It broke her heart that her mom was one of these. One day soon, she would be ready to try to reach her mom. She believed wholeheartedly that, over time, her mom would find a way to let her in and that Emma would be there when she did. She allowed one small tear to make its way down her cheek before she resolutely turned the tears off and pulled herself back to the many items in the plus column.

Overall, Emma really had felt strong and whole and excited about the future. Her dad was right that she had been at a crescendo in her life when she went to sleep that night. Things had definitely been looking up. But she had been scared and worried, too. She had been trying to come to grips with being raped but didn't really know how to do that. In addition, she had doubts that she would ever be great college material and, although she had been excited about her first apartment, there had been apprehension, too, about living alone for the first time in her life.

She saw that for every high, there would be a low, and she knew that growing up would have come at a cost.

She wasn't sure if she would grow up here in AFTER, but she knew that she would grow and, though she felt sad at times, she hadn't felt scared at all since that first day. Truth was, she hadn't even felt particularly tired, and there were so very many times she had been tired on earth.

She knew the word "content" was kind of for adults – people her age weren't supposed to feel content. They had their whole lives ahead of them. They weren't supposed to feel satisfied, arrived, calm, or mellow. Yet these were words that described how she was feeling right now. She felt gratified with life – happy in her own skin in a way that, truly, she had not BEFORE.

As she walked around from room to room experiencing her house without Aunt Pat, she realized how different it felt now that she was alone in it for the first time. It was almost like when she came home for her first semester break from college. Oh, she had been home for weekends here and there, mostly to do her laundry and because she needed a quick family fix. But, when she came home at the end of the semester, it was to stay for a few weeks, and she had brought her pillows and her favorite quilt and the photos she had kept on her desk so that she could set them back up on her nightstand and make her room her own again. Though there had been immense comfort in coming home, there had been a little tension as well. She was once again bound by her parent's rules. She ate what they ate when they ate it, and she had to tell them where she was going and when she would return.

Most of her high school friends had also been home for semester break. Although they had slipped back with ease into the friendships they had before they went away to school, there were traces of the changes that started as they left their own homes for the next phase of their lives. They spoke of new friends and new adventures and new worries, like maintaining grades and picking majors. They were no longer Geneva High School Vikings – they were Michigan State Spartans or Southern Illinois Salukis or Miami University Redhawks. She herself had become an Illinois State University Redbird. *(Good thing! Imagine if I had been a Viking sitting up in that tree at the funeral!)*

Yes, coming home had been the same in so many ways, but subtly different in other ways and, as she walked around the home that she lived in for 19 years, she experienced the same feeling. This was her home and, aside from the awesome changes she supposed she had willed into being, it was the same as it had always been.

But she was bringing a different her to it. It was she who had changed – she who had started to move away from all she had known and everyone she had loved toward a new life that was largely crafted by her. She brought to it all that she had been, but now she had to make her own decisions and face the consequences of her actions without the ready touchstone that her family provided for what was right and what was wrong.

She remembered her father's words at her funeral. He said that she had become, and in many ways he was right. But she knew now that she was still becoming. She realized that she was genuinely excited that her next phase would unfold in this magical place – a place she had only just begun to experience.

It was time, she suddenly realized, to go into her room again. It was the one place she had not been since the day she woke up. It's not that she had been afraid. It's just that, if any place in the world was the symbol of all she had been, it was this room ... the room that had been hers since she was a baby ... the single place in which so many aspects of Emma had been their most intense.

She went up the stairs slowly, taking her time. As she walked down the hall, she observed that there was light spilling out of her room and, as she neared, she felt drawn to it and knew that it was right for her to be here. She stood in the doorway for a minute, amazed as she had been that first morning at the blaze of color and the sense of peace that engulfed her. Once again she noticed that the pictures of her family and friends seemed almost alive, and she could almost hear their whispered greeting, *Welcome back, Emma. It's good to have you home.*

Her bed looked awesome – still piled high with feather mattresses, downy pillows, and soft blankets. She lay down on it and became enveloped in its softness. As she thought back on all that had been, both here and BEFORE, she realized once again that she was blessed. She had been loved on earth, but she was also loved here. She had loved on earth – her family, her friends, her dogs, and her cat. But she also loved here. She had been alive every minute of every day – on earth, she had slept under a sign that said, *Live life to the fullest and embrace it, with no regrets.* It was there now, and Emma smiled.

She settled further into her bed. *I believe I can rest now,* she thought to herself. *It's been a long, long day.* She put her iTunes on shuffle and closed her eyes. There was absolute stillness for several moments and then ... the first song that came on was *The Heart of Life.*

Oh my gosh, she thought, as she started to lose herself in sleep. *Perfect. I wonder if someone actually sent this to me,* she giggled. *Wouldn't that be hilarious?*

As she took the final step into sleep, her last thoughts were of home – a lovely blending of all she had known BEFORE and all she had learned AFTER. And it was good.

Afterword

Emma opened her eyes. The sun streaming through her window was unusually bright, and her room was bursting with color and warmth and vibrancy. She was profoundly happy, although her thoughts were a little muddled. She had images of her family, her friends, Juice ... but they were mixed up with images of Aunt Pat and Grandpa Mebane and Nanna and Grandaddy and Duck. She saw a lovely girl with a pony tail, and she felt the warm glow of friendship as she grappled with a name ... Alice, maybe? *And who was that hot guy?*

As she pulled herself farther out of sleep, Emma realized that these images, which she had initially dismissed as snatches of a dream, felt more real than a dream. They felt almost like memories. She mentally shook herself and tried to remember the real yesterday, tried to connect with having pizza with her brother and her dad and working the counter shift at Town House. But these images had the texture of a dream – they were fuzzy and distant. The longer she lay awake, the more real Alice and Flynn *(yes, that was the hot guy's name)* became.

Gradually, she realized that in her ... dream ... she had died. But had it been a dream? Was she alive and well in Geneva, Illinois, or had she died in this very room, in this very bed? What was now, and what was then? And which way did she want it to be? She knew at the very core of her being that she would never lose her family and the others she had loved over her lifetime. They were a part of her and always would be. But she had a sense that, if she let go of Alice and Flynn and Aunt Pat and Grandpa Mebane, she may lose them forever. She wasn't sure the choice was hers, but she knew that once she got out of bed, there would be no going back.

Just as she was worried that she was thinking so hard she might have a brain cramp, the choice was made for her as Duck jumped up on the bed all wiggly and smiley and looking for love. *Hello boy,* she said and realized she was grinning. *It is so good to see you!*

As she reached across the bed to scratch Duck's ears, her iPad cover slid back and, as she had every morning of every day since Facebook was invented, she checked her News Feed.

There front and center was the picture of her with Sarah and Ben that had been taken right before Mom went to London and which Ben used as his profile picture. Ben hadn't been on Facebook since her funeral, and she was curious why he had gone on today. She immediately saw something that was so monumental that she thought for a second she hadn't seen it right. Ben, her sweet, quiet, introverted brother who had never really had a real girlfriend had changed his status to IN A RELATIONSHIP. *OMG,* she whispered to Duck. *Your boy's in love!* She touched the picture. *Go, Ben,* she said, and she felt a surge of pride both for him and for herself since she had no doubt that this was, at least in part, the result of her handiwork.

She lay there for another few minutes, snuggling with Duck. She thought about what the future might hold, and she decided it was time to venture out beyond Geneva. Maybe today she and Alice should plan a road trip ... Maybe today Flynn would ask her out on a date and they'd go to New York or Dublin or even Paris ... Maybe today she'd go to London and see her mom ... why not? The possibilities were endless.

Then, wondering what today would really bring, she smiled, threw back the covers, and got out of bed.

Author Notes

I'm not a theologian or a psychologist or a philosopher. I'm not even a writer. I'm just a mom who loves my kids and assumed, like every mom does, that they'd be a part of my life for all of my life. But in July 2011, after an evening during which she laughed for hours with her family and helped her best friend prepare for a long-anticipated trip to New York, my beloved daughter, Emma, went to sleep and never woke up. This may not have caused a fissure in the universe, darkened the stars, or stopped all the clocks but, in Geneva, Illinois (a sleepy little Chicago suburb where Emma lived her whole life), the world flipped on its axis.

Emma's death started a journey for literally hundreds of friends, family, friends of family, teachers, coaches, and, on occasion, strangers – all of whom were shocked to lose such a sunny presence in such a bizarre and unthinkable way.

Emma literally relaxed to death. She died in her dreams. And that just doesn't happen to a healthy, vibrant 19-year-old. For years, friends joked that they wanted to be Emma – they wanted her looks, her clothes, her room, and her "party" basement where it seemed every kid in town passed through at least once or twice. They were drawn to her artistic talent, her love of life, and her "shine." They loved her parents and her siblings and her pets. They were envious of her job, her car, her always-state-of-the-art phone and computer. And then she died.

The bottom dropped out of the many lives Emma had touched. Hundreds of friends from every facet of her life came together for her visitation, many staying together for her funeral and a balloon release afterwards. Over the ensuing days and weeks, pockets of people formed spontaneously to remember her, and numerous friends came to Emma's home just to hang out.

Throughout all of this, the great connector was Facebook. Emma's death generated literally thousands of entries expressing a depth of despair not often experienced by people so young. But right from the start, these kids also tried to get at the essential joy of Emma and her absolute love of life. There were pictures and comments and "likes" and poems and songs and tags and links.

For days, every one of her friends replaced their profile pictures with ones of her or with favorite pictures of them together with her. Eventually, her family joined in and then their friends and colleagues. Emma's Wall became an important part of the grieving process and remains pivotal today, so many months after her death.

I read those entries over and over and over during the first months after Emma died. They became my lifeline as I desperately tried to keep breathing and to stave off the darkness that threatened to consume me. I slept fitfully with my iPad in my arms, and I checked Emma's Wall frequently throughout the night and day.

The most common phrase I saw during that time was that "there are no words" – no words that could help with this bottomless and senseless grief – and I readily agreed.

Yet, eventually I came to realize that the countless Facebook words – perhaps due to their sheer volume alone – were starting to make a tiny difference. And, taken together, they gave me a great gift. I began to develop an intimate and detailed understanding of what Emma was like as a friend and a richer sense of the impact she had on the lives of so many people, some of whom I had never even heard of.

And so the seed of an idea was planted. Several of my friends told me that I should write down what I was thinking, and I tried. Unfortunately, my thoughts were dark, devoid of all hope that I would ever find a way to live without my darling baby girl. At some point, the Facebook entries and my rambling notes started to merge, and the seed grew into an idea for a book in which Emma was the heroine, just by being who she was – a funny, friendly, sweet, often confused, but seldom discouraged teenage girl.

Several Facebook entries told of dreams during which Emma visited and brought comfort. People also spoke of songs they believed that Emma sent at just the right moment to signal something special. As with most kids, music was an important part of Emma's life. It was also an important part of her death – we ended her funeral with a slide show set to four of her all-time favorite songs. I started to wonder if perhaps Emma was trying to find ways to stay connected with all of us and to bring what comfort she could through these connections. This became another part of the idea that was growing.

In the spring of 2011, Emma, her beloved siblings – Ben and Sarah – and I started to plan a fabulous vacation that we intended to take in October. After Emma died, Ben opted out, but Sarah and I decided – after much agonizing soul searching, many tears, and endless discussion – that we would still take that trip, hoping we would find some of the peace that had thus far eluded us in our grief. On the recommendation of a well-traveled friend, we selected Kalkan, Turkey, and from the moment our plane landed in that magical place, we knew we made the right choice.

It was on the bus from the airport to our rented villa that ideas of the past months converged, and I suddenly could envision the book that I would write. It would be a book in which Emma "wakes up" on the day she didn't. It would tell of how she experiences her new world, and it would capture her spirit and her sass. It would describe a world with new sets of rules that Emma would surely find a way to break, just as she did on earth! But it would also describe the world that Emma left behind – a world that was new to those who now must learn to live in it without her. Most importantly, it would describe the link between the two worlds and the ways that Emma learns to keep that link strong.

Sarah and I sat down every morning and sketched out the plot for each chapter while we looked out over the sparkling Mediterranean Sea. Sarah talked of feeling Emma's presence regularly throughout that week and, in several spots, including the last chapter, she believed Emma guided us.

As for me, I did feel peace that week and have found it occasionally since as I've written these chapters. Unlike others, however, I have struggled to "feel" Emma. Mostly I just feel sad. There remain no words to describe how much I miss her and the void she has left in my life. Though I think of her every moment of every day, she does not try to connect with me, at least not in ways I can understand.

About midway through the book, I did have a dream about Emma. She was getting ready for a huge, important party. Although she didn't realize it, she was dead, and it was starting to show. She was distraught that she couldn't cover up the marks on her face or style her always-gorgeous-but-now-lifeless hair. She kept begging me for my help to make her beautiful again. I tried and tried, but I couldn't do it. I awoke filled with despair.

A few days later, my sister shared her reactions to what I had written so far of *Tomorrow Comes*. She concluded by saying, "Emma would be so proud that you did this for her." Funny, I thought that I had done it for me. But perhaps it is also for her – for the lasting memories she will leave with others. Perhaps it will diminish the horror and great sadness of her death and intensify the images of the glittery, sparkly, enchanting young lady that she was.

If this turns out to be the case, I hope that I do make my beautiful daughter proud. More than that, I hope that she lives in a place like the one I have envisioned and that she is making new friends and breaking new rules. I hope that the songs we hear truly are sent from her and that, someday, she will find a way to comfort me. Most of all, I hope that when I die we will be together again in the manifestation of Geneva, Illinois, that perhaps she now calls home.

[signature]

Geneva, Illinois

Acknowledgements

The journey from a personal, private reflection on Emma to a book now available for others would not have happened without the loving help, unending support and unwavering belief in me by several people, many of whom became lifelong friends as a result.

The first person outside of my family with whom I shared that I was writing a book was **Mark Sullivan**. Mark had lost his beloved mother just a few days before I lost Emma. Despite his struggle with his own grief – or perhaps because of it – he immediately embraced the ideas I shared about *Tomorrow Comes*. His genuine interest in the book went beyond my concept of it as a vehicle to work through my own grief – he actually wanted to read it himself. Over the weeks following our first conversation, he regularly checked in with me encouraging me to "keep going" and each conversation ended with the words "I can't wait to read this book." I realized that I wanted him to like it ... perhaps the first step from being "just a mom" to being an "author." After all, what makes a writer an author is readers and, from the beginning, Mark held out the warm promise that there would at least be one!

The second person instrumental in this journey was **Sherry Barrat**, at the time the Vice-Chairman of The Northern Trust, a large, global financial services company and my employer. Sherry took time out of her busy schedule to visit me while I was in London, where I had returned to complete my work assignment after Emma's death. In answer to her question about how I was able to find the strength to keep standing, I told her that writing this book was helping just a little. As Mark had been, Sherry was intrigued with the idea and vigorously encouraged me to keep writing. Furthermore, she mentioned people she knew who might help with publication if I should want to consider that at some point. And so the idea was born that there might be multiple readers and a way to reach them. Sherry initiated contact often, always offering words of wisdom and support.

Largely because of Mark and Sherry's encouragement, I decided that I would indeed share Emma's book with a group of friends and colleagues whom I trusted to give me honest feedback without crushing my spirit and erasing any healing that the writing process was facilitating. In addition to Mark (and soon after, his wife, Beth) and Sherry, these "official" reviewers included:

Jennie Barker, herself a new mum and, as such, was worried to read a book about the loss of a child, but did it anyhow ... for me.

Emma Calvert, *the first new friend I made in London and whom we counted on to be objective since "Emma stories" were new to her.*

Mary Farias, *whose no-nonsense editing reduced rambling and added much needed and greatly appreciated professionalism.*

Linda Heinz, *an "unofficial" official reviewer with whom I now have a bond that mothers should never have to share. Linda's response to the book meant the world to me because I know she knows.*

Jean Maglio, *a dear friend and avid reader who, in her dauntless way, moved immediately from support to action, reaching out to others to generate interest in the book and making the first "sale" to a stranger who sat next to her on a plane.*

Annamae Martinez, *another dear friend, whose own terrible losses she rarely talked about until she understood that talking about them would help me. As difficult as it was for her to read this book, I knew she would do it and that her feedback would always be honest.*

Margaret McCabe, *whose willingness to read the book and provide detailed and thoughtful feedback hastened our journey from colleagues to friends.*

Gill Pembleton, *my manager while I was in London, who expanded her unwavering support of me as a person to include a genuine support of this book.*

Kelly Crone and **Christine Smith**, *my sister Carol's friends, who knew none of the Mebanes and so could provide the vital feedback that approximated the reactions of "real" future readers.*

Sarah Rosenstein, my Sarah's best friend, whom we counted on not to be objective because she had known and loved Emma.

Maureen Chambers, another of Sarah's good friends who took the time to love the book despite being a new mom with her hands full of all things Claire.

Jane Reid, whose feedback was so thoughtful it enabled us to see the true themes of the book and to shape them in the hopes that her amazing expectations would be met.

And, finally, my wonderful friend, Sonia Vora, herself a writer and a teacher, who spent countless hours both letting me talk and talk and talk about Tomorrow Comes and gently guiding me in so many ways that made this a better book, a better experience for me, and a better place in which Emma could live on.

In addition, I'd like to thank my other two Northern Trust managers – **Michelle Hoskins**, and the "big" boss, **Tim Moen**. Along with Gill, you helped me create the space I needed to continue to contribute at work, while retaining the energy required to write each evening at home. Thank you for understanding that life is more than work and for providing the environment I needed to work at life again.

Finally, I have two families to thank. First, the Davis family. You taught me to laugh, to love, and to live life to its fullest so that, in turn, I might teach these things to my own children. Thank you. And a special thank you to my sister, Carol. You have taken every step of this journey with me. I am so sorry for your pain and so grateful for your love.

Last but not least, thank you from the bottom of my heart to the Geneva Mebanes, my wonderful family.

Jason, you made me a mom – a gift I will cherish until my own dying breath. You are more important to this family than you realize, and we are grateful that your journeys keep bringing you home.

Ben, thank you, my sweet son, for letting me show the part of you that was such a vital piece of the Emma story. It can't have been easy, and your willingness to do so is a testament to your selflessness and profound love for me and for her.

Sarah, the magic was real. But magic isn't enough, and you knew that. You listened endlessly to every word over and over and always, always made me believe that "it was good." You shaped the book with your insights, your patience, and your thoughtful remembering, and you eased my journey back from the brink with your love.

Rod, bless you for making my reality your own, for doing the hard work, and for the constancy of your humor, your encouragement, and your love. Helping me grow this seed of an idea into a reality fills part of the hole in my heart with laughter and light and goodness. What a gift.

And Emma. Beautiful Emma. You lived a life so large I can almost believe that it continues even better than it was, that your laughter still lights our path, that your love still find its way to our hearts, and that you, blessedly, are somewhere, somehow, still you.

Emma and her mom – June 24, 2011 – London, England

Book Notes

Cover

The silhouetted image on the cover of *Tomorrow Comes* is a combination of Emma, in her junior-year first-day-of-school picture, and Duck, in his ever-ready sentry position. The image was inspired by a photograph shared by Sarah Lee, a colleague from the County of Derbyshire in England. You can find Ms. Lee's original image on <u>starshinegalaxy.com</u>.

The cover as a whole was beautifully designed by Gwyn Snider of Tennessee-based GKS Creative. Jared Kuritz, Managing Partner of STRATEGIES Public Relations, served as cover design consultant.

Trademarks

Tomorrow Comes includes various references to registered trademarks. The marks used and the mark owners are listed below. When the marks are used in the text, the ® symbol is omitted. In addition, if a protected name is used as a verb, it is not capitalized in order to convey colloquial usage. For example, when Emma "googled" a phrase, all lower-case letters are used to describe her action.

Marks Used in the Book – amazon.com®, Kindle®, (Amazon Technologies Inc.), ▊, Facebook® (Facebook Inc.), FaceTime®, iBooks®, iPad®, iPod®, iPhone®, iTunes®

(Apple Inc.), Google® (Google Inc.), HeyTell® (Voxilate Inc.), nook® (BARNESANDNOBLE.COM LLC), Shazam® (Shazam Entertainment Ltd.), Skype® (Microsoft Corp.), StubHub!® (StubHub Inc.), StumbleUpon® (StumbleUpon Inc.), TripAdvisor® (TripAdvisor LLC), and Twitter® (Twitter Inc.).

Fonts

Fontsets used in this print version of *Tomorrow Comes* include: Arial and Arial Narrow, Book Antiqua, Bradley Hand, Caecilia, Calibri, Century Schoolbook, Cordia New, Garamond, Mistral, Palatino, Segoe Script, Times New Roman, Trebuchet, and VAG Rounded.

Copyrighted Works

Quotations included in the text are attributed to these copyrighted works: "Dayman" (from *It's Always Sunny in Philadelphia)*, "Death is Nothing At All" (Henry Scott-Holland), "In the Aeroplane Over the Sea" (Neutral Milk Hotel), "The Heart of Life" (John Mayer), "Star Star" (The Frames), and "Thank Goodness" (from *Wicked)*.

Publication Contact

Activities related to publication of *Tomorrow Comes* are coordinated by R. M. Mebane (the "STARMASTER"). Direct all inquiries to starmaster@starshinegalaxy.com.

If you liked "Tomorrow Comes" you will absolutely LOVE —

A book abot Chaps

by Emma Mebane

PAPERBACK: 20 pages ★ PUBLISHER: Starshine Galaxy
LANGUAGE: First Grade ★ ISBN: 0615520928 ★ $4.95

In first-grade language, *chaps* is pronounced *shapes*. So, this book is about (abot) shapes (chaps). It was written and illustrated in 1998 by Emma Mebane who, as a first grader, was new to the world of *chaps*. But, what Emma lacked in accuracy she made up in spirit – in her bright, bold representation of eight different *chaps,* including the *carkol,* the *dimind,* and the *scwar.*

Emma found her original **Book Abot Chaps** several years ago in one of her mother's "save" piles. With no pride of authorship, she howled at her own goofs in spelling and presentation and shared the book with others, who were equally amused. In the gathering after Emma's untimely death in July 2011, a number of people saw the book and commented on how much they loved it. That sealed its fate as a book destined for greatness.

A Book Abot Chaps, published posthumously in Emma's name, is meant to encourage us to laugh at ourselves, and proceeds of sale support charitable purposes. To obtain a copy, visit <u>starshinegalaxy.com</u> or any of the major online booksellers.